KT-442-737

THE
CITY
GARDEN

Designing & Creating
Outdoor Living Space

THE CITY GARDEN

Designing & Creating
Outdoor Living Space

SUSAN BERRY
Consultant: Anthony Paul

a Salamander book
Published by Salamander Books Limited
LONDON

A SALAMANDER BOOK

Published by Salamander Books Limited
129-137 York Way
London N7 9LG
United Kingdom

1 3 5 7 9 8 6 4 2

© Salamander Books Ltd, 1996

ISBN 0 86101 856 7

All rights reserved. No part of this book may be reproduced, stored in
a retrieval system or transmitted in any form or by any means,
electronic, mechanical, photocopying, recording or otherwise,
without the prior permission of Salamander Books.

All correspondence concerning the content of this volume should be
addressed to Salamander Books Ltd.

CREDITS
Editor: Anne McDowall
Consultant: Anthony Paul
Designer: Bill Mason
Artwork illustrations: Sally Launder
Photographs: The Garden Picture Library
Colour reproduction: Pixel Tech Prepress, Singapore
Printed in Italy

CONTENTS

Foreword

I don't blame gardeners for being confused when they are trying to choose a gardening book. There is a plethora on many subjects but, believe it or not, almost nothing on city gardening. That is until now. *The City Garden* shows not only that gardening in the city can be an enormous amount of rewarding fun and pleasure, but also how to examine every little urban space that is available to make a garden.

But what makes gardening different in the city, I hear you ask? Can't I just bring back a few plants from my next visit to the country? The point is that, because of the lack of space and light, city gardening requires a lot more thought, and in some ways, more design input, than its counterpart, the country garden. This is not to say that city gardening is difficult – it is in fact relatively simple – but you do need to know some basic facts in order to deal effectively with the problems before, or as, they arise.

So often I find that city gardens are neglected because of a lack of knowledge or ideas, and this is particularly true of 'problem' sites. This book contains a wealth of ideas for such spaces, giving advice on, for example, how to convert a dank dark basement into a warm space with pots of lush plants and soft paint colours. There are also suggestions for how to treat balconies, rooftops and alleys, all of which have potential as green or visual areas, and ideas for creating outdoor living space where you can relax and dine 'al fresco'.

Over my twenty five years of practice as a garden designer, I have had great fun solving the problems of hostile conditions for plants – poor soil, lack of sunlight, or dry sun – that are often found in city gardens. I know that many people who have never gardened before regard plants as difficult things that are prone to die, but in fact, with a small amount of care, plants in a city garden can be very rewarding. The secret lies partly in choosing the right plants for your conditions. Experimenting with plants in your garden can be very exciting and rewarding, and gardening itself is a wonderful way to relax.

Many city gardens have miroclimates and, even in temperate regions, suffer little from frost or cold, and they are therefore ideal for growing sub-tropical plants, such as banana plants. Don't be afraid to use good strong-shaped plants – their form will give an immediate strength and vitality to your small space. Many such architectural plants are suitable for containers and so are particularly valuable for the urban dweller.

A city garden is the ideal environment for ornament and colour and you will need to give special thought to such garden features. You can paint all sorts of objects to fill the garden, from bright pots to furniture and trellises, stained, perhaps, in blues and greens. There are also all sorts of more unusual effects you could experiment with, from murals to lengthen the garden to 'trompe l'oeil' doors into the wall, or perhaps a mirror at the back of a water feature. The ideas are endless. My advice is don't be afraid to go for something new – we need inspired gardeners in this world as much as we need to have new ideas in our homes. Finally, remember that the best ideas are usually the simplest ones.

Anthony Paul

▷ This roof garden, attractively screened and sheltered with trellis, plays host to a variety of plants, including a couple of small trees. The water feature on the left, built as a raised pool against one wall, provides a focus of interest, while terracotta pots are both functional and ornamental.

Introduction

▽ York stone flags, interplanted with creeping plants to soften their formality, provide an attractive surface for this small patio, while large-leaved foliage plants, and a raised water feature, provide architectural interest.

Gardening in a city is not the easiest of environments in which to raise plants, but the challenge is part of the fun, and the rewards are immeasurable once your efforts start to bear fruit. By nature of the landscape – with its surroundings of brick, stone and concrete – your garden will stand out like a jewel, provided you plan it with imagination and verve, and tend it with care.

No matter how small the space, you can find something delightful to grow that will give you great pleasure in an otherwise sterile landscape. Even the smallest windowbox will make a successful home for a wide range of plants, and both dark, dingy basements and windswept roof terraces on high-rise blocks of flats can be turned into surprisingly attractive small gardens.

One of the key things to consider when you are designing and planting a small space is what your needs are, and the amount of time and attention you will be able to lavish on the garden. If you are constantly off on holiday or business, it would be a grave mistake to create a garden that needs a lot of attention. Far better, in these circumstances, to opt for a low-maintenance garden, with easy to care for shrubs and ground cover, and some good-quality hard surfacing, so that the garden looks as good on your return as it did on your departure.

Do not be put off by hostile conditions – high walls, limited space, poor-quality soil, or whatever. Plants can be found that will scale most vertical walls, either on their own or with the help of simple supports, or you can fit brackets to the walls and suspend a number of pots from them.

Attractive containers, large or small, in natural materials – stone, terracotta or metal – can be used to house plants if the garden has already been concreted over, or if the soil quality is poor. Plants can be used to screen unsightly views, giving you both much needed privacy and shelter for your more choice plants, and yourselves, from the elements.

The choice of styles for small spaces is

▷ Note how well architectural forms have been balanced in this courtyard garden. The irregular rectangles of York stone, banded by river-washed pebbles, make a sympathetic surface, while the planting, confined to the house walls and to large containers, creates a soft, living frame to the setting.

almost limitless, from the neat, Zen-like efficiency of a Japanese garden, in which natural materials and neatly formed shrubs predominate, to a rampant wilderness of vigorous plants, competing with each other for the available space and light. Scale is not the most important element in success, but using what space there is well is essential. Make the most of what you have, by covering the vertical surfaces with plants, and ensure that you have a good variety of plants for all seasons, since in an urban landscape your garden will be your opportunity to observe these subtle changes throughout the months, keeping you in touch with the natural world.

If you enjoy the contact with nature, try to make the most of it by making your small space a refuge for birds and insects – you will be surprised by how many different kinds even a small garden will attract. A small pond or water feature provides you with an enormous bonus, not only in the range of plants you can grow, but also in the way that it attracts insects and birds, and even exotic-looking dragonflies.

Colour is a great asset in the grey environment of a city, and the plain and simple background of brick, stone and concrete provides an ideal foil for a rich and varied array of flowering plants. If you garden in the countryside, you are, perforce, obliged to plant your garden in harmony with the natural surroundings beyond it, and in a temperate climate this usually means picking a pastel colour palette, as brighter colours tend to jar with too much greenery. In a city garden, you can, if you wish, go for stronger, more Mediterranean colours, and a generally more exotic look, which is well set off by a cool grey stone or concrete backdrop. If you are lucky enough to have brick walls and a reasonable amount of sunlight, you can grow a wide range of sun-loving herbs, with delicious scent and singularly attractive silvery leaves – lavender, rosemary, different kinds of sage, artemisia and senecio are all ideal

◁ Even a small city garden can have a lawn, provided it has a reasonable amount of light. This walled garden contains a mixture of formal and informal elements, with its rectangular box-hedged bed of lavender as the focal point, and the border planting a softer mixture of shrubs and perennials.

▽ Separated as it is from other gardens, a roof terrace gives you plenty of scope to exercise your imagination. This small roof garden has an oriental theme, with its pebble and decking surface, its reed screens, low wooden furniture with spare lines, and its classic bamboos.

candidates for an aromatic, silver-leaved planting scheme.

As anyone knows who has ever walked through the backstreets of Europe and had their eye caught by a single brilliant scarlet geranium framed in a small window, even the smallest space can provide you with a theatrical setting for plants. If you have limited space at your disposal, choosing star performers – like geraniums (correctly called pelargoniums), which have brilliant flower colour over a long season, and require very little attention – is one of the keys to success.

No matter how inhospitable the space you have at your disposal, you will find plants that will grow in it successfully, although your choice may be much more limited. A small shady basement, for example, is not the ideal home for plants, but there are those that will do very well there – particularly plants that have adapted, say, to life in at the bottom of the forest floor where very little light penetrates. (See pages 88-9 for more on plants for shade.)

A garden in a city is not just a place to observe and enjoy nature, it is also a much-needed additional living space, be it a small balcony or verandah, a roof terrace or a patio. If the space you have is large enough to use in this way, then

make the most of it by turning it into an attractive outdoor room. Pick furniture that suits the design, and fits well into it, and use umbrellas and colourful cushions, if you wish, to add warmth and verve to the setting.

Sitting in your small garden, enjoying the dying light as the sun sinks low on a summer evening, can provide a wonderful release from the stresses and strains of city life. A small amount of time spent planning your city garden, and a little time spent caring for it, will be repaid over and over again as you savour its sensual pleasures of scent, colour, life and variety.

FUNCTION & FORM

THE MAIN ELEMENTS that determine the structure of the garden are the vertical and horizontal surfaces – the walls, fences and screening shrubs and trees that define the boundaries and the paved areas, with a variety of materials such as brick, stone, gravel or wood, that form the garden floor. This chapter discusses the various choices at your disposal, and the different ways in which these elements can be treated, or combined to best effect. Remember that it is the combination of all the choices, and the way they harmonize, that will determine the success of your garden design. Keep the colour range limited, of both plants and artefacts, to maximize the space available.

◁ This small roof garden has made excellent use of architectural features, with its neat decking, powder blue painted trelliswork and handsome stone pots of clipped box.

▷ An object lesson in how to combine classical features with planting informality, this small city garden, with its neat brick patio and twisted spirals of box, is softened by trailing ivies, pelargoniums and roses.

The structure of the garden

▽ A pergola adds a much needed vertical element to a city garden, and provides a home for a range of climbing plants, ideally those that flower at different seasons to give you colour, and perhaps even scent, throughout the year.

The key element in planning any garden is to have some idea of the shape you want it to take. All too often, people think only of the plants they would like to grow, without considering the fact that the garden is actually a form of living sculpture, not just a painting – in other words it has a three-dimensional element that you ignore at your peril.

The easiest way to create a satisfying design is to think and plan vertically as well as horizontally. It is the taller elements – bigger shrubs and trees, and walls and fences – which give the garden its defining structure. Once you have this in place, you can then go on to plan how to fill this in. A garden that has no vertical definition looks curiously bleak and monotonous, no matter how attractive the planting within it.

Although large gardens are greatly improved if this internal space is divided up in some way, in very small gardens the aim is often the opposite – to try to create a more unified appearance by theming the garden in some way. You can do this by shape, by colour or by form. Ideally, do not mix too many of these design elements together, otherwise the garden will seem bitty, confused and much smaller than it actually is.

▷ A simple but stylish solution for a long garden, the punctuation point of the conifers at the end of the vista helps to enclose the space and foreshorten it. Rich red bricks for the paved area make a good contrast with the architectural formality of the planting, much of it in clipped evergreens.

In a city garden, the surrounds to it are crucially important – you will find it far more delightful if it feels private and personal, or as private and personal as you can make it. It is worth adding height to the fences by using trellis to grow climbers, or by adding a couple of tall, slender trees in a small garden to blot out an unattractive view. Even a typical small city plot no bigger than 13.7 x 5.5m (45 x 18ft) can still play host to three or four small trees, and it is well worth while including at least two if your garden has none. Not only will it give you some privacy, but it will also give the garden a pocket of shade where you can grow different plants. Not all plants enjoy the same conditions, and the more varied your garden situation is, the greater opportunity you have for creating varied planting interest.

Small hedges can help to provide a feeling of division in the garden without breaking up the area too greatly, and box hedges are ideal for defining small formal areas of the garden, especially if you mix them with some softer looser planting to soften their severity of shape and line.

Remember that the floor of the garden is equally important, and as a first priority, do ensure that whatever covers the garden – be it stone, concrete

or grass – is suitable for your needs. It is very difficult to make much of any flat, monotonous surface, so if a previous owner has concreted over your garden, consider either laying another more attractive surface over it (timber decking for example) or dividing up the whole area and removing some of the concrete to create larger beds.

△ This small square courtyard has been given a greater sense of space and privacy by compartmentalizing it, using climbers to cover pergolas and arches. Low boxed hedges enclose and define planted areas, the design centering around a small formal pool.

Paving

▽ Large flagstones provide the surface interest in this small parterre-style patio. Clipped box provides the vertical features, and the white-painted cane furniture, and garden gate, add a touch of light.

▷ This narrow alley garden has employed quarry tiles for the surface, echoing the detailing in the brickwork over the gateway. In a dark setting like this, a bright surface provides a splash of colour and warmth.

Your garden may already have some form of paving – all too often rather unattractive expanses of concrete – or you may decide to create a patio area outside your back door where you can sit and enjoy the garden at your leisure. It is worth considering carefully the various choices of paving that you can make.

Natural stone

One of the most beautiful paving materials is natural stone. It has a deceptively soft-looking texture and colour, which blends perfectly with almost any style of planting, from formal to sprawling cottage-style plantings. Its beauty is not without a price, however – it is the most expensive of all forms of surfacing – but it is definitely a great asset in any garden, if you can afford it.

As with any hard surface, it must be properly laid to ensure it presents an even surface. Normally, the ground will have to be dug over, and then the soil tamped down. A footing will be needed of hardcore (broken bits of rubble), over which sand is laid. The stone flags are then laid in the sand, which is also used to fill the gaps between the flags. Naturally, the slabs are heavy, and you will probably find it worthwhile to get them professionally laid.

Concrete

Cheaper paved surfaces include concrete flags. These days you can buy concrete flags that imitate real stone ones. Some of the best ones have a slightly warm colouring in imitation sandstone colours, with a slightly rough hewn surface.

When you lay the stones you can choose to butt them up tight together, or to lay them with fairly wide gaps, in which you can plant some little perennials, such as thymes. These will survive happily when crushed underfoot, and release a wonderful scent in the process. Small paving plants, such as *Acaena buchananii* or *Viola riviniana* 'Purpurea', or even the larger *Alchemilla mollis*, will selfseed happily in the cracks, quickly helping to give new paving an air of permanence. A particularly pretty little self-seeding daisy, *Erigeron karvinskianus*, will

provide clouds of small rose pink to white flowers in summer, spilling over walls and down steps.

Another trick is to lay the slabs like a chequerboard, infilling the spaces with either gravel or a tough grass. Alternatively, you could leave occasional spaces in which to plant a large mound-forming shrub or perennial – the big handsome *Euphorbia characias wulfenii* or a sprawling *Brachyglottis* 'Sunshine' will both relax over the paving.

Alternatively, you can mix stone with other hard-surfacing materials to break up any monotonous appearance that a single surface would give. Bricks could be laid as a course around the paving stones, for example, or large pebbles could be used to fill any irregular shapes that the square format of the stones would naturally leave. Much depends on the size and shape of the space that is being paved, and it is not a good idea in a very small area to create too bitty a design. A more uniform paving design will help increase the apparent space.

However, that being said, it is often a good idea to use a different paving material for distinctly different areas – for example the long alley down one side of a terraced house could be laid with recycled bricks and the patio area of the garden paved with York stone.

Bricks

Of all the hard-surfacing materials, brick is arguably the most attractive. It wears reasonably well (although not as well as stone), and it has a wonderfully rich warmth and colour, especially as it ages and weathers. It blends with most architectural styles, and with almost any kind of planting scheme, formal or informal. Containers in terracotta are an ideal partner for brick surfaces, the natural soft earth tones of the terracotta picking up the russet colour of the bricks. Try large pots of hydrangeas or neatly clipped box balls to mark each end of a path, for example.

Similar to bricks, but made of different materials, are granite setts and paviors. These are a steely blue grey in colour and can look rather severe unless the garden is planted up to alleviate it. A colour scheme in pale pastel shades – whites, pinks and blues – will help to bring a feeling of lightness to such a surface. Granite can work extremely well with modern architecture, where brick, for example, might look rather too rustic. It is important to match the paving surface for the garden to the architectural style and materials of the house. It will give the area unity and help you to feel that the garden flows naturally out from the house itself.

Bricks are, of course, rather more time-consuming to lay than paving flags, but you can also be very inventive in the forms and patterns that the bricks take, using circles, crescents or different rectangular laying patterns, such as herringbone or basketweave. You could, for example, define the sitting area of the garden with a large brick circle, the bricks radiating out like the spokes of a wheel. This works very well with a low-maintenance shrub and perennial planting surrounding it, in which the plants – big bushes of lavender, rosemary, viburnum and hydrangeas, for example, spill out, softening the edges of the brick area.

◁ Brick paving provides the flooring solution for this small courtyard garden, echoing the brickwork of the surrounding house and walls,which have been painted white to create the maximum reflection of light. Grouping the planting adds to the emphasis.

▽ A wonderful swirling pattern of bricks and granite setts makes a real feature of the surface of this small Dutch garden. Note how the spokes of the umbrella echo the form of the brickwork.

Laying bricks

Laying bricks, as with paving stones, requires careful preparation of the site if the bricks are not to sink. First you need to ensure that the site is completely level. This is normally done with string and posts. You will then need to prepare the ground, tamp the soil down firmly, lay a good thick hardcore base, about lOcm (2in) deep, with a 5cm (2in) layer of sand on top into which the bricks are set. The bricks should be laid to butt up to each other and sand then brushed into the joints between them. Edges can be created with bricks set on edge, sunk slightly deeper than the adjoining bricks of the main paved area. Alternatively, you can lay the bricks at a 45 degree angle to create an interesting edge.

Bricks with other materials

Bricks are also ideal for edging other paved surfaces, such as stone or granite setts. You can make thin string courses surrounding a whole paved area or around each individual group of stones, to make a chequerboard pattern.

A circular design can be very effective for a small sitting or dining area, either as a full circle or as a half one. A cheaper variation on the brick and granite sett surface shown right would be to create a gravel circle edged by a double or triple layer of bricks.

Timber surfaces

▽ Timber and gravel make excellent partners for an informal path. The effect is softened here by creeping and sprawling plants.

More recent in origin than stone or bricks as a surface for the garden, decking is widely used in countries that have a natural supply of timber, and is increasingly being adopted as a surface in city gardens by garden designers, who find its flexibility a great asset. It is relatively easy to lay, durable, and easy to maintain, provided you spend the money on a good hardwood, such as teak, for example, which will need nothing more than a once a year scrub with a stiff brush and some fungicide. Softwood decking will also need regular treatment with a wood preservative .

Decking produces a wonderfully soft-looking surface, which can be left natural or stained in one of the good new colours now available – slate blue, silvery grey or a soft bottle green all make a good foil for the planting. Stronger colours would be too strident and dominant.

Decking will cope particularly well with an uneven site, saving you from spending a lot of money levelling it out. You simply adjust the height of the bearing timbers to take in any changes of level. In fact, you can use any changes of level to your advantage to build a tiered or stepped surface, which helps add interest to the garden. If you want to include a water feature in a small

▷ This little roof garden has been surfaced with diagonally laid decking, painted battleship blue-grey. Wooden decking makes an excellent surface for roof gardens, but take care to ensure that any moisture-proof membrane is not pierced while it is being laid.

garden, decking is an ideal medium to use, as you can incorporate the pond into the decked area, building the decked surface over part of the pond to form a bridge.

As it is relatively light, decking is also one of the best surfaces for a roof terrace. The main concern here is not to pierce any damp-proof membrane covering the roof terrace in the construction of a new surface, but as the roof-top surface is already flat, you can simply 'float' the decking a few centimetres above the asphalt on reasonably heavy load-bearing joists. Always check with a building surveyor when planning a roof terrace, or any work to it, to ensure that it will not only bear the weight of whatever you have in mind, but also that any drainage system that exists is adequate for the purpose.

Railway sleepers

Another option is to use recycled railway sleepers, which work well used along with another hard surface material, such as stone or gravel. Laid diagonally, these sleepers can form an interesting surface with plenty of textural variety. Be warned, however, that the timber can become slippery unless scrubbed at least once a year with fungicide. Railway sleepers also make very good surrounds for raised beds, in a simple box-like construction, which would work well with a timber and stone surface pattern.

A raised deck of large railway sleepers could also be used to define a small sitting area at the end, say, of a bricked patio, and looks very good with some of the modern, sturdy all-weather teak garden furniture.

△ To relieve any feeling of monotony over a large surface area, the decking here has been laid with different contours, each change of contour marked with a different direction of the decking. Bold architectural foliage plants add to the oriental feel.

Paths and steps

▽ Steps can be more than just a convenience – wide steps like these provide an opportunity for planting, particularly in pots, arranged, as these are, in architecturally pleasing formation. Small pots of geraniums are ideal for this purpose.

△Steps can be attractively softened using creeping plants that flourish in dry, stony soil. Alchemilla mollis and baby's tears (*Soleirolia soleirolii*) are both good candidates for this kind of situation.

All too often, paths and steps are neglected in small gardens, which is a great shame, as they provide a wonderful opportunity for novel planting ideas. If you are lucky enough to have a flight of steps leading down to a small garden, then make sure you use them to full advantage. If there is enough room, you could put a small container on each step, each containing the same kind and colour of plant – for example, chrysanthemums or small terracotta pots of bulbs in spring, pelargoniums in summer, or even neatly clipped little box balls or pyramids for all year round architectural splendour. Alternatively, use the steps as a support for an attractive climber – the golden leaved hop (*Humulus lupulus* 'Aureus') or an attractive variegated ivy for example, or even a small flowered clematis, such as one of the viticella types.

Shallow flights of wider steps can be planted at the sides with sprawling plants, such as some of the spreading forms of cotoneaster, or any of the daisy family. Alternatively, persuade one of the self-seeding perennials, such as the little bellflower (*Campanula*

◁ The effect of a mini tropical jungle can be created quite easily with appropriate planting of large-leaved foliage plants and sympathetic treatment of hard surfaces – here pebbles with a stepping stone path, and timber decking and bridging. Hostas, ligularis and bamboos are good choices for this effect.

▽ Small changes of contour and direction can be used creatively, as here, to make shallow steps. Mixing surface materials, such as flagstones and bricks, helps to add interest, and is in keeping with the attractive informality of the perennial planting.

portenschlagiana) to make its home on the steps. These little campanulas are notorious for finding the smallest crack in which to seed themselves. Other good self-seeders for shade are some of the small common ferns, which look wonderful growing alongside brick or stone in a narrow-ribbon like display.

Paths can be made from a wide range of surfacing materials, including the usual stone and timber, but gravel and wood paths are also attractive, particularly for an oriental-style garden. You can set round flat cross-sections of timber into a gravel path, as stepping stones, or use railway sleeper as insets, rather like a railway track, into the gravel (see pages 20-1).

Be careful when planning steps for a city garden that they are sufficiently wide to be functional if you are going to be carrying equipment, or trays of food, up and down into the garden. The same applies to steps onto a roof terrace, for example. Simple wooden steps can be constructed easily and simply from a couple of thick planks of wood, coated with preservative.

Walls, fences and screens

◁ A high wall, whether of the house or garden, provides a home for the vigorous *Wisteria floribunda*, with its long racemes of lilac flowers, which appear in late spring.

▷To avoid monotony, the boundary fence for this garden has been given a mixed treatment with a wood panel fence, arranged vertically, topped with square painted trellis. Painting trellis not only helps preserve it, it creates interest while any climbing plants are growing to cover it.

The surrounds to the garden are extremely important in a city, where privacy and shelter are essential pre-requisites to enjoying your garden. If you are lucky enough to have a walled garden, you can use this as an attractive backdrop for the planting. A few masonry nails and wires will provide adequate support for a range of twining climbers that will offer an enticing display of flowers throughout the year. Clematis, climbing roses, honeysuckles, *Solanum crispum,* and jasmines are all ideal candidates, as are some of the wall shrubs, such as *Fremontodendron californicum,* with its large yellow cup-shaped flowers, and *Carpenteria californica,* with its glossy evergreen leaves and sparkling white flowers with a yellow eye.

A low wall can be increased in height by attaching trellis to the upper part, over which you can encourage the climbers to grow. This not only gives you privacy, but with any luck will deter marauding neighbourhood cats.

If the walls around your garden are made of an unattractive material, disguise them firstly by painting them a more appropriate colour – a rich deep green for example – and, secondly, by growing plants over and against them.

Fences

Fences in most city gardens need to be secure and fairly tough, both for security and for protection. Make sure that any lapboard fences are supported with well-sunk stout upright timbers at close intervals – normally about every l.8m (6ft) apart. Again, the height can be extended using trellis, which, unlike lapboard fencing, does not act like a sail in a high wind, and is therefore less likely to blow down.

▷ This attractive wooden screen, painted a delicate sage green, makes an excellent foil for the handsome Alibaba pot. Painting screens in toning colours is an ideal way to harmonize the surfaces with the planting.

Screens

Screens of any kind are vital for sitting areas, both on a small patio and on an exposed balcony or roof terrace. Bear in mind that if the wind can permeate the screen to some extent it will create less of a problem than a completely weatherproof form. For areas that are exposed to high winds, consider constructing your own trellis from sturdy timber, at least 2.5cm (1in) in section, pre–treated with preservative. You can create any pattern you like and you can stain the trellis in any one of a number of appealing natural wood stains, or in a soft pastel shade.

For roof gardens and balconies, you might like to use bamboo or reed

◁ A hot tub – a small heated pool sunk into the terrace – has long been popular in warmer climates and it can make a wonderfully relaxing addition to a city garden, provided it is screened to provide some privacy for the users, as here. Decking is the ideal surface into which to set a hot tub, as it provides both a comfortable surface underfoot and an easy means of setting the tub into the surrounding area.

▷ Reed or bamboo screens, although not immensely long lasting, provide an excellent solution for temporary screening, being attractive and inexpensive, and sympathetic to both architectural features and planting.

screens, popular in oriental gardens since time immemorial. Similar forms can be found made from willow, hazel or brushwood. Although not as long lasting as trellis, they are a good solution for a city garden, and most will last a minimum of five years. As with trellis, you will need to attach the screens to firmly fixed, sufficiently strong supports.

Using trees and shrubs

In a small city patio garden, some of the most necessary screening is to hide unattractive views. A judiciously placed, reasonably fast-growing tree can often blot out an eyesore, such as a tall block of flats. A columnar tree, such as *Chamaecyparis lawsoniana*, will work well for this purpose. The golden form 'Ellwoodii' is more attractive than the plain green species.

Even a delicate birch tree, while not completely blanking off an unattractive view, will help to diffuse it, while at the same time allowing quite a lot of light into the garden, which is sometimes a very important requirement in a small city patio, which might otherwise become too shaded.

Some plants can make excellent screens for coastal towns, where salty winds can wreak havoc in the garden. Consider using either elaeagnus or grisellinia as an evergreen screen. Both will cope

extremely well with pollution as well as salt-spray, and they can be clipped to make a good weatherproof hedge.

Other good screening plants are privet, box and yew. A single large shrub can provide a useful screen for a small garden shed in a little city patio, and low hedges of shrubs such as lavender, rosemary and box can be used to divide and compartmentalize even the smallest town garden.

Screens can be useful in a small city garden to hide any storage, such as a small garden shed, or, if you are

ecologically minded, a compost heap. A large bushy shrub will serve the purpose well – *Elaeagnus* x *ebbingei* makes a good solid evergreen screen, is quite fast growing, and has the bonus of scented, but inconspicuous flowers, in autumn. Alternatively, use trellis and grow evergreen climbers, such as *Hydrangea anomala petiolaris* or one of the more attractive ivies, over it. Variegated holly will make an excellent screen, but most are not very quick growing and will take a while before they begin to serve the purpose you have in mind.

Choosing A Style

Your choice of garden style is dictated by the shape, situation and aspect as much as by personal choice. In this chapter, the principal types of garden are discussed, from small city balconies to larger outdoor rooms, from narrow shady alleyways that run up the side of the house to purpose-built roof gardens. It includes advice on the different ways to construct, plan and plant these so that you make best use of the aspect, and the available light or prevailing conditions. City gardens can take on many guises; you are not obliged to opt for slick formality; a small junge-like oasis, or even a wild garden, are just as welcome as a neatly paved rectangle of patio. Make sure, however, that your choice reflects your lifestyle, and can be maintained with ease in the time you have available to you.

◁ This simply planted, walled city garden has used vertical surfaces for climbers, with a small water feature as a focal point in the gravelled patio area. Mound-forming perennials soften the hard surfaces.

▷ Attractive York stone paving, and an abundance of containers, with topiary, daisies, pelargoniums and patio roses, make this small backyard a delightful oasis.

Basements & small patios

▽ Two big pots of marguerites mark the division between a narrow alley and the garden. Stargazer lilies, petunias, hydrangeas and pelargoniums create a splash of colour in a shady corner.

When you have a very limited space at your disposal, you will need to think very carefully about how to make best use of it. Normally in a city environment, any small gardening space is bound to be overshadowed by the buildings that surround it, so at least half your energy and effort will be spent on ways to make the best use of shaded areas.

If you have a tall wall bordering your small garden, you will need to get as much light as you can to be reflected into the space. Painting a grey concrete or dark brick wall white is the obvious solution to creating greater reflectivity. This, in turn, has an obvious effect on the design, as a plain white backdrop is not normally found in nature, and your design will have to make the most of this rather Mediterranean-style setting.

The best solution is to use the wall to grow climbers on it, either by attaching trellis to the wall or by using wires attached to masonry nails. The climbers you choose will be determined, to a large degree, by the quality of the light and the direction the garden faces, as well as by how dry or damp the area is. Any area with a high wall is normally dry in the shadow of it, so by and large you are likely to need plants that thrive in these conditions, as well as ones that cope with the high alkaline content

▷ This simple design has a central pond as its focal point. The choice of hard surface could be decking, paving, bricks or flags, as appropriate for your situation and your budget. A couple of borders provide the permanent planting, while pots and containers, which can be moved as necessary, provide colour and interest throughout the year.

▽ This little brick-paved basement garden uses architectural features and foliage plants to make up for the lack of light, in a formalized design.

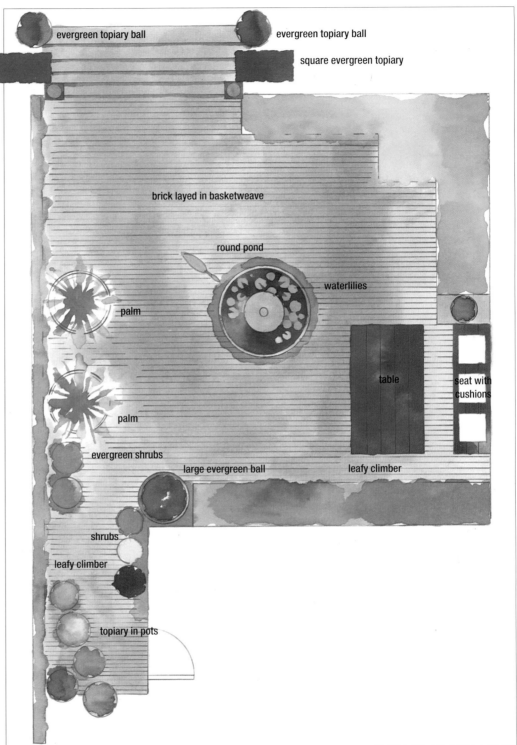

evergreen topiary ball

evergreen topiary ball

square evergreen topiary

brick layed in basketweave

round pond

waterlilies

palm

palm

table

seat with cushions

evergreen shrubs

large evergreen ball

leafy climber

shrubs

leafy climber

topiary in pots

usually left behind by quantities of builder's rubble. Clematis will thrive in dry alkaline soil, but does need some light. *C. montana* is one of the toughest species, and will cope with a north- or east-facing wall, covering it in spring with myriad small starry flowers in white or pink, depending on the variety.

Ivies are the obvious choice for any basement walls, since they will tolerate even quite deep shade, although the variegated forms, particularly those with gold-splashed leaves, such as 'Goldheart', need more light to retain the variegation. *Hydrangea anomala petiolaris* will thrive on a north wall, but is not keen on very dry soil ('hydra' means water), so unless the area is

▽ The handsome metal spiral staircase, leading down to the basement patio, makes a feature in its own right. Shade-loving plants, including hostas and ferns, create the backbone of the planting, with ivy clothing the walls.

naturally damp or you are prepared to do a lot of watering in dry weather, you might do best to give this one a miss.

Be careful in these kinds of conditions that the soil has enough nutrients in it to keep the plants going, as there may well be very little decaying plant matter going back into the soil to feed it, and it is therefore down to you, the gardener, to supply it, in generous amounts. There are plenty of proprietary fertilizers to choose from, and if your plants are failing to grow well, or bloom when they should, inadequate feeding, and watering, are the most likely causes, apart from lack of light.

In a small area, apart from covering the vertical surfaces with plants to increase the available growing area, it will pay to group the plants together. You get a commensurably greater effect from three plants grouped together in a single display than you do from ten dotted around in a haphazard way. Also, do not be deceived into thinking that because the space is very small, you must only grow very small plants. One large plant of exceptional beauty in a handsome container is worth 20 of no special merit. If you pick a plant with attractive evergreen foliage, and make sure it is growing well and healthily in a large attractive container, it will form a focus for a small basement or patio. You

◁ The distinguishing features of this small enclosed garden are the choice of surface – natural stone, river-washed pebbles and tiles, laid assymetrically. Screening trellis and a trompe l'oeil arch provide vertical interest, and grouped displays of plants in terracotta pots soften the architectural features.

▽ Every inch of available space has been used in this narrow basement, with the stairs making a home for colourful containers of busy lizzies, pelargoniums and lobelia.The walls can be used to provide colour, not only by using climbing plants, but by hanging wall pots or troughs on them.

can surround it with a changing display of smaller plants for spring and summer colour if you wish.

If the area is overlooked from indoors, try to use the space to give yourself something of particular interest right through the year, picking scented plants, or those that flower in winter, as well as those for summer display, as your small garden is going to be your sole contact with the changing seasons. Containers are particularly useful, as they allow you to move and change the display as plants come in and out of flower. If you organize your planting carefully, you can group bulbs in a container with smaller plants, thereby giving yourself a display of spring bulbs, followed by perennials in summer, for example. One good choice might be early flowering narcissus with a display of small alliums for summer.

In addition to using any available wall space for growing climbers, you can also hang wall pots (containers with a curved front and straight back) on the walls, and fill them with trailing annuals, such as busy lizzies, trailing pelargoniums, lobelia, diascia and nasturtiums. Ideally, keep the planting colour themed to prevent it looking too bitty and busy. Busy lizzies will cope very well with low light levels and are therefore handy for dark basements.

Alleys & narrow spaces

▷ This shady small garden makes excellent use of natural woodland plants, including ferns, pulmonarias and foxgloves, to create a wonderfully dappled secret garden. The use of natural stone for the path is a sympathetic choice.

▽ This narrow garden makes good use of containers and handsome garden ornaments, including a circular stone table and gothic chairs, sculptures and terracotta pots.

In some city gardens, behind terraced houses, there is a long finger of land that runs alongside the back of the property. All too often, this is an overlooked planting area, which is a great shame, as space is limited and it offers great potential for some inspired design solutions.

First of all, consider the surfacing. If it is just concreted over, why not lay ceramic tiles or perhaps wooden decking over it to create a more sympathetic look. Deep red and black quarry tiles are sometimes used in this situation, and provide the key design point for a Victorian-style planting scheme, concentrating on ferns and other evergreens – perhaps formally clipped box balls or pyramids in terracotta pots – as the permanent display, with other container-grown plants brought in to enliven the scheme in spring and summer. *Zantedeschia aethiopica*, the big arum, with its shiny green leaves and brilliant white spathes, will make a good clump and you can divide the plants to increase your stock. They do well in the shady conditions that often prevail, but they will need plenty of humus and a regular and plentiful supply of water. Some spring bulbs – 'Paper White' narcissi, in single displays in shallow pots, perhaps, or several small pots of snowdrops – would

look good in this setting. If there is room, consider putting a narrow table against a wall or fence to act as a permanent display base.

Use the walls to hang wall pots or containers, but try to keep the display with a fairly defined colour palette, and make sure the pots are attractive in their own right, and combine well together. Rather than scatter them over the wall, why not position four or five together in a group, perhaps with a large container nearby with a handsome vine, such as *Vitis coignetiae*, whose large, heart-shaped leaves will make an attractive

display for most of the year, before turning a wonderful glowing russet in autumn.

If you decide to give this area a wooden decked surface, then you could also build in some large wooden containers – either square Versailles tubs with neatly clipped geometrically shaped evergreens or low-level window box-style containers. This is particularly useful if the soil in this area has been concreted over. A decked area can have a slightly softer planting scheme, perhaps using more sprawling plants, but again they will have to be able to tolerate a degree of shade. Consider using several different kinds of ivy, perhaps with a *Fatsia japonica* if there is room. Lower level window boxes could be planted with ferns, hostas and busy lizzies, along with some small ivies.

A sculpture or other garden ornament – such as a single, large, handsome terracotta pot – can provide a focal element at the end of a long passageway, and will look good with an end wall as a backdrop for it. Statues look particularly attractive when half hidden in creepers, either ivy or parthenocissus, for example. Smaller plants that tolerate a degree of shade, such as corydalis, small, tough campanulas and *Viola riviniana* 'Purpurea', are good for softening the edges of paving.

▽ By offsetting the path at an angle, this narrow space is optically widenened, its edges softened with creeping plants. Long spaces can be improved by grouping pots together at intervals to divert the eye.

Pathways and entrances

Long narrow areas can also be found around pathways and entrances, and here, especially, it is important to create planting schemes that frame the space attractively and give it some kind of punctuation point. Pairs of pots are ideal for marking the entrance to a house or garden, and they can be either architectural and formal looking, or loosely composed and sprawling. In summer, a pair of large pots of the big Regale lily make a wonderful way to mark the entrance to the garden, and the rich perfume is strong enough to drift in through open windows and doors. In autumn, you could replace these with pots of large white chrysanthemums, and in spring, with the glistening tall white tulip, 'Triumphator'.

In sunnier narrow spaces, you could mark the edges of a walkway with clipped bushes of lavender, santolina or artemisia, all of them fragrant and with silvery foliage. Blue, pink and white flowers go well with silver-grey foliage and salvias, dianthus, *Lychnis coronaria* (in the pink or white form) and with soft velvety leaves, or scented tobacco plants, in white or deep pink, would all fit well with this kind of planting scheme. You could also edge sunny paths and walkways with low clipped

▷ A long alleyway can be transformed into a magical woodland walk with relatively simple design features – in this case a path of offset stepping stones, planted with shrubs, trees and shade-loving perennials.

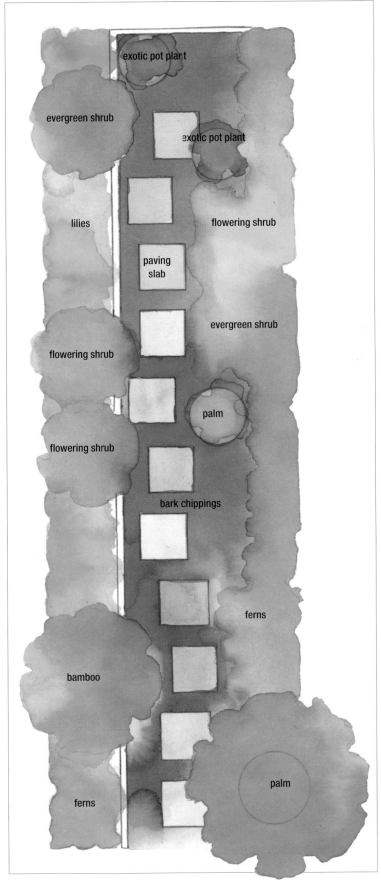

exotic pot plant

evergreen shrub

exotic pot plant

lilies

flowering shrub

paving slab

evergreen shrub

flowering shrub

palm

flowering shrub

bark chippings

ferns

bamboo

palm

ferns

hedges of box (*Buxus sempervirens*), which is also aromatic. A large pot of one of the summer daisies, such as *Leucanthemum vulgare*, the ox–eye daisy, with a sprawling display, makes a good counterpoint to the neatly clipped hedges, as do some of the flowering climbers, such as violet or white clematis, or white and pale pink climbing roses.

Make sure any doors, gates and other woodwork is painted or stained in sympathetic shades of soft blues, steely greys, and bluish greens, so that they present a harmonious picture. Be careful not to include brilliant white tubs or pots in this kind of setting – they make too obvious a statement.

△ This little alleyway, with its stepping stones of brick set in bark chippings, the raised beds held with stout wooden planks, and its handsome large-leaved evergreens, makes a delightful, secluded woodland walk.

Roof gardens

▽ This little roof garden has made sympathetic use of wood with its decked surface and wooden planters. A low level screen of plants helps to provide shelter without destroying the beauty of the rooftop view.

Many newly converted flats are now boasting small roof gardens, but the problem of creating a private, sheltered and attractive garden on a very exposed site can be daunting to the newcomer to gardening, who may never have grown anything at all before.

The garden will not create an inviting place for either plants or people unless you create some shelter from the prevailing winds, both to protect you and the plants, and to give you some very necessary privacy. There is a wide range of ways in which you can do this, but since you will certainly also want to enjoy the view, you will need to find some kind of compromise.

▽ Decking makes an excellent choice of surface for a roof terrace, since the material is natural and sympathetic, and easy to lay on existing foundations. Here the planting has been largely confined to troughs around the perimeter of the terrace, to increase the feeling of space.

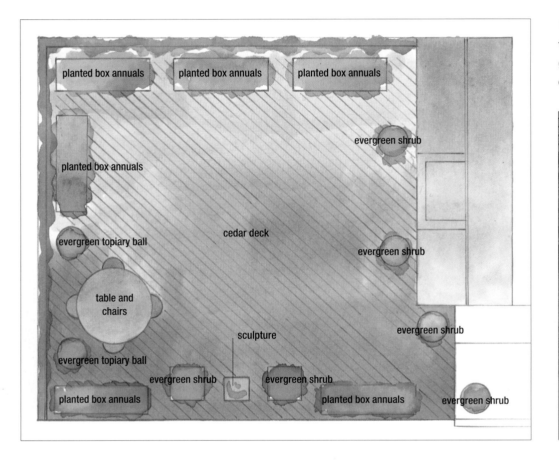

▽ Duck-egg blue trellis blends attractively with the natural wooden decked floor of this roof garden. Wooden planters and terracotta pots create a home for sun-loving perennials.

The best solution is to opt for a mixture of screening and planting that provides a partial rather than a complete screen. The wind will be able to penetrate such a structure to some degree, which will prevent the whole thing acting like a sail and taking off in high winds. Nevertheless, any trellis that you use as a support for plants must be very firmly anchored at the base, and must be reasonably solid in construction.

Remember that the vertical aspect of a roof garden will have to be constructed by you, and without it the garden will look bleak no matter how colourful it is. Aim to include at least a couple of large shrubs in pots or even a couple of small trees, such as bay tree, perhaps, or a weeping cherry or birch. Make sure the screening is covered with a variety of attractive climbers, ideally flowering at different times of year – honeysuckles, clematis, jasmines and roses are all possibilities for the roof terrace. For something more unusual, consider the passionflower (*Passiflora caerulea*) or the kiwi fruit (*Actinidia kolomikta*).

It is essential to get the roof surveyed to check whether its load-bearing capacity is adequate for the garden design you have in mind. Weight is always a problem for roof gardens, as you will have to import soil in which to grow plants, and this is not light. On the whole, the areas around the edge of a roof are the strongest, and this is therefore usually the best place to site large or heavy containers.

Drainage is also a key factor to consider, as rain water and any surplus from watering must be able to soak away without damaging the property. You will need to install adequate drainage, if there is none already, and

an impermeable surface is, of course, a necessity. Over the top of this, you can use a more sympathetic surface such as teak decking, but make sure that you do not pierce any waterproof membranes during construction.

A small pool is always a possibility on a roof garden, provided, again, that the load-bearing timbers are up to coping with the weight. A small half-barrel – perhaps housing a few irises, *Pontederia*

cordata, and even a miniature water lily – makes an ideal little water garden. To fill the pool, and to water the garden, which will need frequent attention in hot climates, you must have a handy supply of water, and it is worth getting a tap fitted on the roof to save you time and energy carrying water upstairs.

Some unusual and exciting roof gardens have been created in some very unprepossessing spaces. Flights of fancy

can be more successful here than on a standard garden plot where the surrounding gardens bring you back to reality with a jolt.

If your roof top is awkwardly shaped and with little space for you to sit out, consider grouping containers together with some interesting mixed planting, wherever the possibility presents itself, to create a mini-jungle. Make sure the displays have a good mixture of foliage

◁ Tiles make an excellent choice of surface for a roof garden, as they are easy to keep clean and attractive in their own right. Here the planting has concentrated mainly on architectural evergreens, leaving the tiles themselves to make the major colour statement.

▽ A monochromatic colour scheme, basically white and green, has been chosen for this part-shaded roof garden. Evergreen climbers, foliage plants and topiary provide the planting interest.

and flowering plants of different shapes and sizes. Some good candidates in pots would be *Fatsia japonica*, *Choisya ternata*, small azaleas (in an acid-based soil mix), a camellia or two, and a couple of climbers, such as a passion flower (*Passiflora caerulea*) and a golden hop (*Humulus lupulus* 'Aurea') as well as a couple of clipped box balls or cones to add formality.

If the space is more rectangular, and open, then you could consider opting for a formal design, such as a Japanese garden, using bamboos in pots, clipped evergreens, mound-forming plants, such as the Yakushimanum azaleas, *Viburnum davidii*, and some of the hebes, with gravel for the surface, and some simple, low tables and chairs in rough hewn wood, perhaps. A bamboo or reed screen panelling could provide the necessary shelter with a suitably oriental feel. Keep the colours fairly subdued so that the eye concentrates most on the architectural shapes, with perhaps just one or two flowering shrubs – such as a large hydrangea – as a focal point.

The whole point of a roof terrace is to allow you to enjoy any good weather, so make sure you leave enough space for at least a couple of chairs, a table and, ideally, a pergola with climbing plants over it to give you some shade.

Balconies & terraces

▽ A profusion of flowering annuals, growing over every inch of vertical space, gives this small balcony a wonderfully secluded feel. Using the balcony railings on which to hang planters helps to increase the planting space.

For many people, a small balcony or terrace, perhaps very little more than a window ledge, is the only space available in which to exercise their horticultural talents. However, it is surprising what you can grow in a very limited space, if you wish to, and how attractive you can make a small balcony or terrace look. Since the area is small, attention is focused on every detail and you will need to make sure that plants are in good condition, and also that the containers are handsome in their own right. Nothing looks worse than a balcony in which a few mismatched, stained plastic pots create a junkyard of half-dying plants!

First of all examine the space you have available, and look at the structure. Decide what will fit along the base, and what you might grow up the wall behind the balcony or terrace, up any supporting poles, and across or over any railings or fences. Then decide whether the balcony is large enough for you to use, or whether it is to perform simply as a display space for plants. The surface requirements (as for a roof terrace) are such that it must be solid, waterproof and free draining, and able to bear the weight of any pots complete with soil. Even lightweight modern composts are heavy when waterlogged, so do be sure that you have assessed this correctly, and if in any doubt seek professional advice. Another factor on balconies is safety: make sure that none of your pots can be blown onto people or gardens below – even heavy pots can be gusted away in high winds.

You can go for a full-blown cottage look or you can opt for something more restrained and formal. The latter is the best option if you're not a keen gardener, as you can create a handsome-looking planting scheme using evergreens, with just a few flowers to add colour if you wish. If you keep the planting symmetrical, simple and balanced, framing doorways with pairs of pots, and lining the base of the balcony with a ribbon planting of, say, pansies, tulips, or busy lizzies in a window box, the space will seem larger and better organized.

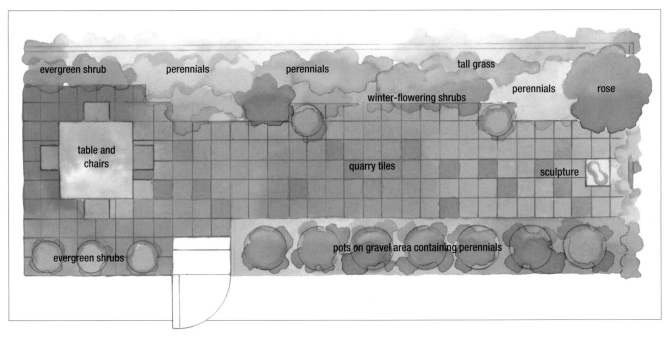

evergreen shrub   perennials   perennials   tall grass

winter-flowering shrubs   perennials   rose

table and chairs

quarry tiles

sculpture

evergreen shrubs

pots on gravel area containing perennials

◁ A long narrow balcony has been given an air of privacy with fairly dense planting both along the back wall adjoining the house and at the front of the balcony, using both floor-level planters and troughs attached to the railings. More space has been allowed at one end to accommodate a table and chairs.

Alternatively, you can amaze the beholder with a veritable hanging garden, created by attaching hanging baskets and wall pots to the walls behind the balcony, fixing window boxes to railings, and using a large range of climbing and trailing plants in addition to perennials and shrubs. Some singularly wonderful gardens have been created on a horizontal growing space no more than a metre wide and a few metres long, using every bit of wall space and railing that surrounds the area. Trailing pelargoniums are excellent for this purpose, as provided they are given some lightweight trellis, they will rapidly clothe a whole wall with a summer-long succession of flowers. Ivies, nasturtiums, diascia and lobelia will all cascade over the edges of hanging baskets, troughs and windowboxes, creating curtains of flowering plants.

In order to maintain a major flowering display over a long period, you will need to water the plants frequently and copiously, and to feed them. To cope with high wall-mounted pots, you will almost certainly need to adapt a garden hose by attaching the last metre

▷ Flower power is not always necessary to obtain a richly planted atmosphere. Here foliage plants – principally acers, cornus, euonymus and ivies – have been used to great effect to create a delightfully cool and verdant scheme.

or so to a garden cane. It takes very little time for a hanging basket to dry out, and for the plants to suffer, so if you are opting for this kind of display, make sure that you have the time to keep it in pristine condition – in midsummer, hanging baskets may well need watering twice a day.

On the whole, simple displays, using a limited colour theme, are the most

effective solution for small balconies and terraces, but climbers are ideal, and many will grow in surprisingly small containers. For example, an ornamental vine will do well in a small wooden barrel, and you can use the same barrel for spring-flowering bulbs – say crocuses or scillas – and, in summer, for a display of sweet peas, which can be encouraged to scramble up the vine.

▷ A small balcony, with formal wrought-iron railings, demands a similarly formal planting scheme. Clipped box, in pompoms, balls, spires or cones, is ideal for the purpose. Flowering annuals can be added in summer for seasonal colour.

◁ This little balcony has a beautifully laid decked surface with planters containing drought-loving plants, such as rosemary, santolina and yuccas. If your balcony is exposed and sunny, as this one is, choose plants that naturally cope in hot dry conditions, otherwise watering will become a chore. Mediterranean plants are among the best choices for this kind of situation.

Making dual use of containers is an excellent solution to limited space, and successional plantings of this kind are ideal, particularly with bulbs, where the bigger bulbs are planted below the level of smaller ones. For example, you could plant crocuses and snowdrops at one level, daffodils at the next, and summer-flowering lilies and alliums below these. Use metal plant labels to remind yourself what you have planted where.

Try to ensure that you have a few scented plants on a balcony, so that their perfume will waft in through any open windows. Honeysuckles are wonderfully scented, and cope well with relatively poor soil, and there is even a winter flowering one, *Lonicera* x *purpusii*. A couple of clematis, such as *C. armandii* and *C. montana*, are scented too, so go for these in preference to the other types. To attract birds and bees to the balcony, train a couple of berrying shrubs, such as pyracantha or cotoneaster, against the wall of the house, perhaps in a neat frame around the window. Large pots of lavender – you could use a neatly clipped pair – will also help attract bees.

No balcony in a city should be without a pot of herbs, and you can grow a few mixed together in one large terracotta pot. Thyme, rosemary, sage, mint and basil are among the best. These days you can buy purpose-made herb pots with compartments, so that you can keep those with a tendency to stray, like mint, firmly confined in their place. Also essential in summer are pelargoniums, which are the easiest to grow of all container plants, requiring almost no attention whatsoever – they suffer only when overwatered. There are some wonderful different kinds to grow, some with wonderfully aromatic leaves. It is a good idea of grow a few different kinds, including upright bushy pelargoniums and the trailing forms mentioned earlier. They are among the easiest of all plants to propagate, and grow rapidly to maturity. If you pinch out the growing tips of young plants, you will get a much more satisfactory bushy plant the following year. However, remember that you cannot overwinter pelargoniums out of doors in colder climates, so make sure there is enough space indoors on window sills to house your collection once the frosts arrive.

A few small evergreens will help to give structure to any display on a balcony. Choose either small forms of conifers, such as some of the dwarf forms of chamaecyparis, or else clip box or bay into neat shapes. Young skimmias, with their smooth glossy dark green leaves, are also good, and as they are slow growing, it will be some time before they become too large for their surroundings.

Formal gardens

▽ This stunning formal patio
has been designed to echo the
surrounding architecture, its
key components of gravel,
water and evergreen planting
all classical formal features.

Very small gardens are often best laid out in quite a strict formal style. There are several reasons why a formal design works well for city gardens – firstly, the architecture of the house forms the backdrop to the garden, and a formal style, with its straight lines and neat box-like construction, echoes this built environment that it surrounds. Secondly, the simplicity of a formal arrangement helps to make the most of the limited space.

Formal gardens were originally designed in France in the eighteenth century by garden architects such as André le Nôtre, the aim being to order nature and tame it. The chief attributes were rectangular beds, straight paths and a neat symmetry about the planting. Translated onto a small plot, the French parterre concept can be juggled slightly to create a similarly styled, but rather more free, design style, with small box hedges, for example, and gravel or brick paths, surrounding small, formally laid out beds. If you are lucky enough to have a reasonable amount of sun, you could grow an interesting range of herbs in the beds between the box hedges. A visit to any good herb garden will give you some good ideas of what to grow, and how to grow it.

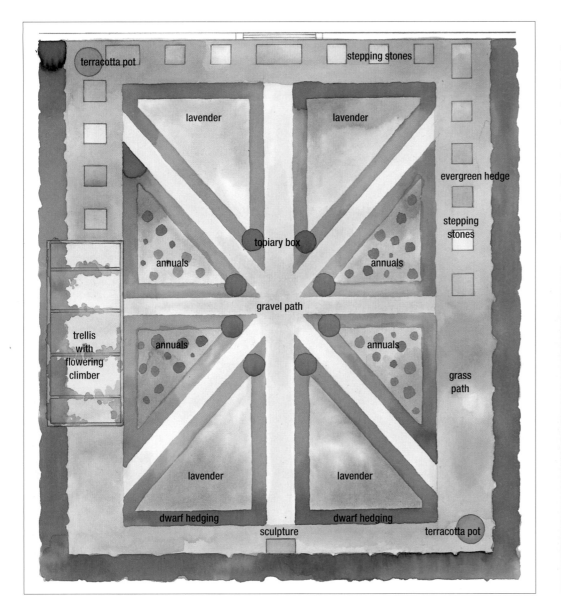

- terracotta pot
- stepping stones
- lavender
- lavender
- evergreen hedge
- topiary box
- stepping stones
- annuals
- annuals
- gravel path
- trellis with flowering climber
- annuals
- annuals
- grass path
- lavender
- lavender
- dwarf hedging
- dwarf hedging
- sculpture
- terracotta pot

◁ This Union-Jack shaped formal garden is an excellent choice for a small rectangular plot. Low box hedges define the compartments, which can be filled with perennials; herbs are the classic choice, but you could also use massed plantings of one kind of plant to achieve a themed display.

▽ This star-shaped, box-edged, herb-filled parterre is an object lesson in formal design, the neat little topiary box pyramids at each corner providing an effective punctuation point, while the statue at the far end creates the focus.

Keeping the colour palette limited and restrained is one of the keys to formal gardening, which tends to make good use of architectural shapes and simple green, gold and white colour themes. Topiary – where slow-growing evergreens are clipped into geometrical shapes – is one of the mainstays of formal gardening, and can be copied on even the smallest city plot. Even a window sill can provide a home for a soldierly row of small terracotta pots, each containing a single clipped box (*Buxus sempervirens*) making a neat, round ball shape.

Repeated plantings, in either ribbon formations, or squares, is another hallmark of formal gardening. It makes planning the garden relatively simple, and provided you are prepared to do some simple propagating yourself, you will be able to stock the garden fairly easily and cheaply. Some shrubs, for example, take very easily from cuttings. Rosemary and box both strike very readily from half-ripe cuttings; simply push them into good compost in a large container, potting them up into individual containers once they have rooted – in roughly three months' time.

Water features are popularly used in formal gardens, often in the form of channels or conduits rather than the free-formed pools most of us associate with garden ponds. In a small city garden, a rectangular pool or small water channel will fit most successfully.

Equally attractive for small formal gardens are pebble pools or splash pools, as are spouts or masks mounted on a wall, which pour water into a raised pool. The sound of a splashing fountain or spout is extremely soothing, and makes a wonderful counterpoint to the formality of the rest of the garden.

Japanese-style gardens

If you grow a good range of evergreen shrubs, you can create a garden that has a formal core to the design, but with an oriental flavour to it. Japanese garden design is extremely formal, but in a rather different vein from the symmetrical lines of French formal gardening. In a Japanese garden, the focus is on the shape and form of the plants themselves and their relationship with the space that surrounds them. Rocks, sand, gravel and pebbles all play their part in formal Japanese design, and this can work well in a city landscape, with quiet steely greys and sober greens harmonizing beautifully with the surrounding buildings.

Modern garden designers have poached many of the concepts of the Japanese garden and adapted the style for Western tastes. Although frowned on by purists, it nevertheless represents an attainable, and attractive, style of gardening. If you like this kind of architectural simplicity, the goal is less rather than more. Choose plants that make a strong architectural statement in their own right, and think carefully about where, and how, you site them. It is important to make sure that the plants are strong, and well grown, since attention is more focused upon them. Arrange the garden with certain clear

focal points in mind, siting the plants at strategic points in the garden , such as at the end of a path or in front of a window.

Statuary and ornament
Statuary and ornament are ideal in a formal garden, and a path or small walkway will often lead towards a single ornament – perhaps a bust on a plinth – sited with care at the end of it. In a small square plot, a large container, or a statue, may be used as the pivotal point around which a series of four rectangular beds are laid out. Again, as in any formal design, remember that less is more; one decent statue, even if it is reproduction rather than antique, will have far more impact than several of lesser quality. Even a simple ornament can be effective – an old chimney pot, perhaps, or some other architectural relic – provided it is well positioned. An alcove in an end wall, or a trellis arch, could be used as a backdrop for it.

Garden rooms

▽ This small, sunny gravel and stone surfaced garden has an interestingly assymetric design, which helps to create a feeling of space in a small plot.

One of the greatest joys of possessing a garden in a city is being able to sit outside surrounded by both plants and wildlife. The sound of water, birdsong or humming insects can be a great bonus in an urban landscape, and it is worth ensuring, provided your garden is large enough to house a couple of chairs, that you can sit out-of-doors when the weather allows.

To this end, plan for a small patio or paved area in the part of the garden that gets the most sunshine. This does not necessarily have to be the part closest to the house, although it is obviously convenient if it is, so that you can carry out drinks and food easily. If, though, your garden faces north and the area behind the house is shaded, then why not site the patio at the far end of the garden, perhaps linking it to the house with a specially created, and planted walkway? If you pave the patio area with a sympathetic surface – be it decking, paving or bricks – you will have a level, even surface on which to site a table and a few chairs.

The planting around any seating area should serve the following ends: it should screen you so as to give you some privacy, shelter you from any prevailing winds, shield you from the intrusiveness of city noise and pollution, and, ideally,

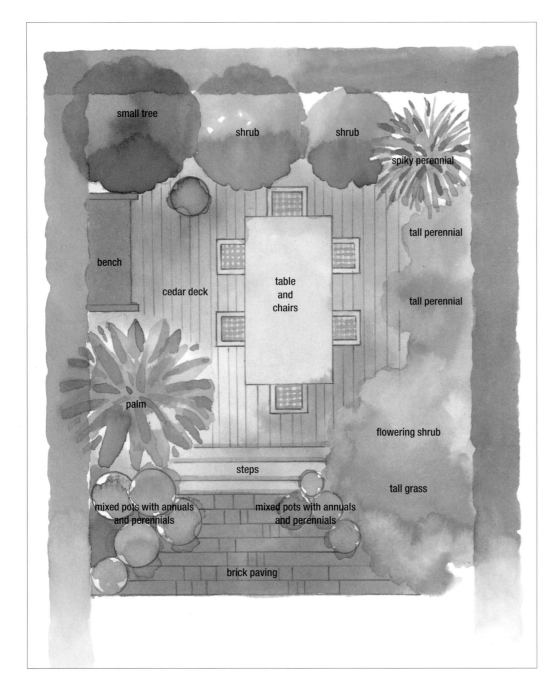

small tree

shrub

shrub

spiky perennial

tall perennial

bench

cedar deck

table
and
chairs

tall perennial

palm

flowering shrub

steps

tall grass

mixed pots with annuals
and perennials

mixed pots with annuals
and perennials

brick paving

◁ This enclosed small space makes
an ideal garden room. A shallow flight
of steps leads up to the sitting area,
which has been attractively screened
with shrubs and trees. Collections of
containers flank the flight of steps,
and provide themed colour in the
summer months.

▽ A raised deck, whether used to cope with a change of
contour or simply as a design feature, helps give a garden
interest, especially when it is lushly planted with some
handsome architectural plants, such as the Abyssinian
banana plant, *Ensete ventricosum*, shown here (left).

offer some shade in very hot weather. If
at all possible, the plants you choose
should give you the bonus of scent, too.
A pergola or trellis is ideal, since it will
give the benefit of partial shade, plus a
support for whatever climbing plants
you might wish to grow.

In southern Europe, no small outdoor
space is complete without a vine, its
large leaves giving wonderful dappled
overhead shade in summer. Even in

colder countries, vines can be used for
the same purpose, although
ornamental, as opposed to fruiting,
vines might be more appropriate. *Vitis
coignetiae* performs well in most
conditions and has handsome large
leaves that turn a wonderful ruby red in
autumn. Combine it with a scented
climber, such as a jasmine, honeysuckle
or rose, and perhaps another for flower
power, such as one of the large-flowered

clematis. A couple of large pots to either
side of the seating area – containing
hydrangeas, perhaps, or ligularias – and
your outdoor room will provide you
with a perfect place to relax and enjoy
whatever quiet moments you can grab.
It will greatly extend your use of the
garden if you light it in the evenings. If
you do not want to install an electrical
supply to the garden, flares or candles
can be used instead to good effect.

◁ Gravel is a relatively inexpensive and very relaxed surface to use for an outdoor room and combines well with most architectural forms. The surrounding planting depends on the situation – foliage plants for shade and sun-loving perennials, sprawling over the gravel, in hot spots.

▽ This delightfully secluded outdoor room, which has been created on a small roof garden, presents a harmonious picture with its emphasis on natural wood, for the floor, trellis screens and decking.

Furniture and furnishings

If you don't want to erect and plant up a pergola, then you can opt instead for one of the large new umbrellas. Among the most attractive are the large, natural umbrellas in bleached canvas-weave cotton with wooden supports. They are sturdy, long-lasting and look particularly good with a decked patio surface and attractive well-built teak furniture (see also pages 64-7). Bring the umbrella in at the end of the summer season and scrub it well before drying it and folding it away.

Do not be tempted to economize on the furniture or furnishings. They will have to last a long time, and the sturdier and better made they are, the better they will withstand the ravages of the city environment. Ideally, choose all-weather furniture that you can leave out all year round, as most houses and flats have little storage room to spare. The furniture should be scrubbed in the spring with a stiff scrubbing brush and some household detergent, and then rinsed off with clean water before leaving it to dry naturally. A pot scourer will remove any stubborn lichen stains, but take care not rub so hard that you damage the wood.

If your garden is too small to accommodate a full-sized table and chairs, then consider positioning a garden bench at a suitable point where you can sit and enjoy some particular delight – whether it is a large container of wonderfully scented summer lilies, or nestling beneath the canopy of an attractive small tree or climber. Benches vary in size and scale, and a tiny iron bench will fit snugly against a wall in even the narrowest small plot.

Access and views

If you are considering using your garden as an outdoor room, then give some thought to the access. It may be worth your while to alter an existing window to make new access to the garden in the form of French windows, so that not only can you move in and out more easily, but also the scents and sounds of the garden will enter the house when the doors are left open. The view from main living room windows is important, and when planning the garden, you should take account of the main vantage points, framing your design accordingly.

In some town houses, the living room window looks down a long narrow finger of land beside the house, and all too often this becomes a messy storage area rather than a feature of the garden. As this is the gateway to the garden itself, and possibly your only view of it, do plan this area into the garden, even if it is not the principal sitting area. A simple planting scheme at ground level (it is likely to be shady) with an attractive hard surface is all that is required, plus some pots and containers that can be changed as the seasons alter, both at ground level and perhaps fixed to any wall or fence surrounding it .

GARDEN FEATURES

IN ADDITION TO THE PLANTS, and the basic structural elements, most gardens are enhanced by a range of special features including pools and fountains, lighting, garden ornaments, garden furniture and overhead screening. The range and choice available to you is enormous, but you have to decide how to make best use of these features in the confined space of the city garden. In this chapter, every kind of water feature is looked at, from small pebble ponds to splashing wall fountains, the different styles and types of furniture to suit every conceivable need and taste, as well as more decorative features, from judiciously placed ornaments to subtle lighting effects.

◁ This small formal water feature, with its raised pond and fountain spout, enhances a shady corner of a small city garden.

▷ A painted bench creates a focus of interest in small semi-formal garden, with its containers of box and sculptured lawn set among an unusual pink, purple and green planting scheme.

Water features

Even the smallest city garden is large enough for a water feature. With its light-reflecting properties, water will appear to enlarge the space rather than reduce it, and you can choose from a whole range of sizes and shapes, from a small sink sunk into the soil to a water feature that takes up most of the available space in the garden. Even in the tiniest, shadiest back yard, you can incorporate an attractive water feature, for example by mounting a mask on a wall (like the one shown above) which drips or pours water into a small pool below – either a simple cistern or tank, or a small raised pool, or even a shallow pebble splash pool, if you prefer.

As with any garden feature, a pool must be in sympathy with the rest of the design. If you have opted for a formal garden, stick to a formal shape for the water feature – a channel or rectangular pool, for example. If your garden has a more cottage feel to it, you can make a naturally shaped pebble pool or shallow irregularly shaped water feature.

Water gardens, surprisingly, are low maintenance, so if you are not too keen on gardening, and enjoy the sight and sound of water, why not think about creating a large water feature, even if you have only a very small site. The surrounding area can be decked to create a seating area, with bridges over a water feature that could, perhaps, fill the whole width of the plot. Many Dutch gardens, where water is an inescapable part of the natural landscape, are constructed around this kind of theme, and it is ideally suited to city gardening.

If your city garden has more than one level to it, you could use these changes in levels to create a cascade leading down to your pool, and install water pumps to circulate the water back up to the top again.

A small fountain is a great delight in a city garden; not only is it attractive to look at, but also the sound of splashing water is extremely soothing.

◁ A pretty little water feature in soft ochre, its fish sculpture spouting water into the raised pool below, makes an ideal feature for a small courtyard garden.

▽ Water can take the form of canals or streams, rather than ponds, running down one side of the garden, as here. A raised walkway, here of brick and decking, makes the ideal viewing platform.

Pool surrounds

The surroundings to the water feature are an important part of its whole appeal. However you choose to construct your pool, make sure that it is edged with suitable material and planted up appropriately. Certain plants flourish in nature in naturally damp and waterlogged conditions, and a pond will only occur in nature where the ground retains moisture. You are not so limited in your own garden, but nothing looks more garish than seeing an artificially constructed pool surrounded by plants that naturally love dry sun – generally silver-leaved plants with bright flowers. The larger, more leafy foliage plants that tend to seed themselves in damp situations will definitely create a more natural, appealing surround to your pool.

If you do not want to edge your pool with a formal hard surface, and you have opted for a shallow pool, then a pebble beach effect at one end of the feature can look very effective. Plants such as *Caltha palustris*, *Trollius europaeus* and *Astilboides tabularis* make excellent poolside plants for this kind of situation, as do the candelabra primulas, various ferns, and a tough geranium, *Geranium macrorrhizum*. Japanese ornaments –including small buddhas nestling in ferns or ivy, or the

typical Japanese deer-scarer, in which a reed pipe trickles water into a container – go well with this kind of look.

If you want to opt for the more formal canal-style water feature, then consider including some other interesting features – perhaps a small Gothic bridge over the water, a little Chinese pavilion, or just a couple of log stepping stones or a simple stone bridge, depending on the size and scale of the garden.

Stepping stones and bridges

There are many ways to create crossings over water features, depending on the size and scale of the feature. For a shallow pool, you might include some stepping stones, for example. These can take the form of single slabs of York stone, or sawn off and treated rounds of timber, or even small constructed squares of teak decking. Make sure you lay them in an inviting and interesting formation rather than in a regular straight line.

◁ For a more naturally planted garden, decking is the ideal companion for a large water feature, in particular because you can bridge the water easily and successfully using it. The overlap of the wooden decking masks the edges of the pond, so that the water seems to flow beneath it.

▽ Water is a key feature in oriental garden design, and it has been used very successfully in this small town garden to give an illusion of space, with its pebble shores, stone bridges and stepping stones.

Very simple bridges can be constructed from just a couple of thick planks bridging two hard surfaces, or they can be supported on simple thick timber joists. Fancier bridges, with handrails, and steps to provide an arch, can also be used if space and style permit.

Ponds for fish and wildlife

If you want to keep fish, you should allow approximately 1800cm^2 (2ft^2) of water surface area to 15cm (6in) of body length (excluding the tail), and koi carp will need a large pond and a water depth of at least 1.2-1.5m (4-5ft). The deeper the pond, at least at one end, the better the survival chances of the fish. You will need to ensure any pond for fish has plenty of oxygenating plants to keep the water fresh, and you will have to feed them yourself in the summer months. In colder weather, their metabolism slows down and they live largely off their own body fat.

If part of your aim in having a pool is to have, or encourage, wildlife in the garden, then you will need to consider their requirements. Birds and small animals need to be able to reach the water easily, so the pool should incorporate a shallow area at one end. Any pond for wildlife should have some natural cover around the edges of the pond, and at least a few plants growing in the water; reeds, irises, Pontederia, and marsh marigolds are ideal. Deeper water will provide a home for water lilies.

Bog gardens

If you do not want a full-scale water feature, you can always opt for a bog garden, giving yourself the chance to grow some unusual and attractive plants through manipulating the soil conditions. If you sink a black plastic liner about a metre beneath the surface, puncturing the base in places to allow drainage holes, you will create an area where the soil retains more moisture than normal, thus allowing you to grow some handsome water-loving plants – rodgersias, ligularias, hostas, the big ornamental rhubarb (*Rheum palmatum*) and even a *Gunnera manicata* – the huge-leaved perennial from Brazil. The latter is slightly tender and will need to have its crowns wrapped in winter in colder climates, but it will make a wonderful architectural feature in the garden during the spring and summer months, growing to a good two or three metres (6-8ft) or more.

Pergolas, arches & canopies

In any small city garden, it pays to include some overhead structure to provide both privacy and shade, and a support for climbing or scrambling plants. There is a wide range of such supporting structures to choose from, from the highly ornate to the remarkably simple. How big and how grand you wish to make such a feature is a matter of taste, and also of budget, but even a relatively simple structure can provide a home for a rich array of plants which can be encouraged to scramble and twine themselves over and around both the vertical and the horizontal elements.

For a very basic structure, sink metal or wooden posts well into the ground to give them strength, and tie, screw or nail overhead horizontal posts or rails to them. For a more rustic form you could use ropes as the horizontal elements, slotting them through eyes on the upright posts.

Often, some kind of seating is included beneath the pergola as it makes such a pleasant place to sit. If you prefer, you can create a smaller structure using one of the garden walls as the back support, so that you have shelter on one side at least. It will make a particularly attractive frame, similar to a bower, for a bench, and if you grow attractive climbers – ideally those that are scented as well as offering attractive flowers – around it, it will be the perfect place to relax on a summer's day. (See pages 98-101 for lists of scented plants.)

Arches

Arches can be used in various ways, but are ideal for framing the entrance to a part of the garden. In a small city garden, an arch could mark the transition from an alleyway to the garden proper. If the area is not sunny enough to grow the usual range of flowering climbers, then train ivies or creepers over it instead, which will give it an architectural grandeur. If you wish, you can add further arches and make a small ivy-clad tunnel, clipping the ivy back once a year to keep it under control. Or position an arch next to the back door, growing whatever takes your fancy over it.

◁ Trelliswork, here in a sturdy pergola surrounding the seating area of this patio, helps to give privacy and shelter to the plants. Well designed pergolas are an architectural ornament in their own right, and do not necessarily need to be planted.

▽ Arches are ideal for framing the entrance to a part of the garden. Here, a metal arch, painted a delicate blue grey, has been used as a support for wisteria, its racemes of delicate mauve flowers drooping attractively from it.

Climbing plants

The aim for most of these structures is to create a canopy of foliage and flowers as quickly as possible. Roses are ideal candidates for pergolas, and most people like to have at least a few with different flowering qualities to receive the full benefit of flowers and scent. The 'Albertine' rose – a vigorous, pretty pale pink rose, and richly scented – is very popular for growing over supports. Other good candidates are the 'English roses' grown by David Austen and the beautifully scented old-fashioned roses.

Make sure that at least one of the plants you choose has attractive foliage – an ornamental vine would be ideal, as would the pretty golden leaved hop, *Humulus lupulus* 'Aureus'. Honeysuckle is particularly good because it smells so delicious, and some forms are semi-evergreen, which will ensure that the structure is clad with leaves all year long. Another good subject is the almond-scented *Clematis armandii,* which also has attractive leathery elongated dark-green leaves, and the passionflower, with its whorls of evergreen leaves and curious blue and white angular-looking flowers.

△ A classical pergola, a small statue on a plinth at the base of each support, makes a focal point in this small city garden. Foliage plants around the base, and hanging baskets containing summer annuals, soften the outlines and help it to blend with the rest of the garden.

Awnings and umbrellas

▽ A canvas awning extends the shelter from the sun in this small corner patio. Awnings are ideal if you already have a supporting vertical structure in place from which to stretch them.

In a city garden, you can use the space much as you would a room in the house, with soft furnishings adding colour and interest, as well as providing protection from the elements. Awnings and canopies can be used to provide much-needed privacy and seclusion, particularly if you have a ground-floor flat and garden, and the garden is overlooked by other tenants occupying the floors above you.

There are various possibilities for covering the ceiling of the garden, including the partial shade afforded by pergolas (see pages 58-9). Large canvas umbrellas, imported from the Far East, have become very popular recently and are fortunately still relatively cheap. For something larger, you could support sailcloth strips on posts with stout string ties. You will, however, need some rapid means of removing these or lowering them to a vertical position in the event of rain, otherwise they will fill up with rain water and tear loose from their moorings under the weight. You could also use very lightweight muslin, rather like mosquito netting, to create a summer awning, or a range of hand-dyed cottons in earthy colours – saffrons, terracottas and burnt oranges.

Reed screens are another possibility for overhead shade. They are relatively light and very easy to fix in position to

◁ A large canvas umbrella, in white or offwhite, looks particularly smart and is also effective. With its sturdy supporting pole and spokes, it offers a much better solution, in both design and functional terms, than the ubiquitous floral parasols so often used for this purpose.

timber supporting struts and posts. You can, if you wish, grow climbers and creepers over them. In normal climatic conditions, they will last for around five years, but as they are relatively inexpensive, it is not a great problem to replace them when they wear.

Fabric can be a wonderful source of colour in the garden and there are a myriad ways to employ it to jazz up the appearance of a dull city garden. The most obvious application is for

colourful cushions – for seats and as floor cushions, if you have decked your patio area with timber – and tablecloths. These kinds of colourful additions work particularly well in shady gardens, which have very little natural colour of their own and benefit enormously from the addition of some imported brightness.

Many people have transformed their living space by stealing a portion of the garden to create a conservatory. If you

do not want the full cost of a conservatory, you can make yourself a lean-to shelter with open sides and a roof of clear PVC. Beware that in a city this is inclined to get dirty, and if it is not to look gimcrack, you do need to give it a good annual scrubbing down. If the posts are painted a deep green, and you grow some interesting climbing plants up them, you can turn this into a surprisingly effective loggia for the spring and summer months.

Garden furniture

▽ When positioning a bench in the garden, it pays to consider its setting carefully. A screening arbour of trellis creates a feeling of privacy and seclusion for this traditional-style bench.

There is, today, no shortage of good garden furniture to choose from. Manufacturers have created some excellent ranges of outdoor furniture from a variety of natural materials, much of it now imported relatively cheaply from the Far East. Wood is one of the most durable and most sympathetic materials, and there is a wide range of furniture types from which to choose, from classic reproductions to modern designs. Since the furniture has to stay out in all weathers, it pays to buy the best you can afford, as it will undoubtedly last better and longer. For this purpose you need a good-quality hardwood, such as teak, which will cope with all weather conditions. Cheaper softwood needs annual coats of preservative to prevent it rotting.

Painted metal garden furniture also looks good – the idiom borrowed from the French with their classic dark green circular fretwork tables and round-seated café chairs with bent backs looking good in most city gardens. Beware opting for white – it gets grimy very quickly in a city. Dark green or slatey blue are better options on the whole. There is also a wide range of cast-iron furniture, some in quite ornate designs. Because it is very heavy, it has the virtue that it does not collapse

or fall over easily, but it is difficult to move around the garden, which can be problem if you want to use more than one area for sitting out.

If you do not see what you want in the shops, there is nothing to stop you designing and making your own simple

furniture. Plain benches or tables, for example, are relatively easy to construct, or you could use a hewn log or railway sleepers to make a simple bench. If you are furnishing the garden on a budget, then hunt out bargains in junk shops and unify any disparity in design by

painting them in matching, or toning, colours. Even plastic furniture can be painted, and you can transform an old white plastic chair into something perfectly acceptable if the basic shape is attractive. Interesting industrial relics can make attractive patio furniture – the base of an old sewing machine can be topped with a piece of marble to serve as a small table, for example.

If you are planning to eat out of doors, it is worth remembering that you need a reasonable amount of space to do so. For a table and chairs for four people, you will need at least 1.5 sq m (16 sq ft) of space, to allow you room to pull back the chairs from the table. A good solution if you want to eat out of doors in a small garden is a bench, a table and a couple of folding chairs for guests. The slatted French café chairs are ideal for this purpose, as they fold up very small and are easily stackable.

It is important in small spaces, such as balconies, verandahs or roof terraces, to pick furniture that fits well into the available space. Folding furniture certainly comes into its own here, as do benches that fit snugly against a wall, for example. If you are at all handy at carpentry, why not make a small table that is hinged to the back wall of the balcony or terrace, so that you can fold it down when not in use.

Lounging furniture

In most small gardens there is not a great deal of space for serious relaxation, nor, frankly, does city life encourage one to spend hours in the garden. However, a few good chairs that enable you to put your feet up while enjoying the vista you have created are a great bonus to a more relaxed lifestyle.

Among the most attractive lounging chairs are the 'steamer' chairs first developed for luxury cruises and now sold in many good department stores. They have the architectural lines of a standard upright chair with the addition of an elongated leg rest. In natural hardwood, such as teak, and furnished with attractive boxed cushions in natural fabrics, such as linen and sailcloth, they make a worthy addition to any outdoor room.

The good old-fashioned deck chair is an excellent standby for the small garden. It folds up to take up minimum space and if the fabric used for it is of good quality, it will last extremely well. There is a wide range of suitable furnishing fabrics, and you can easily revamp old deck chairs with any strong sailcloth or canvas fabric.

▽ Good-quality, well-designed sturdy garden furniture is not cheap, but it is a worthwhile investment, and functional too. It will last well, and show remarkably little sign of wear and tear. A once a year scrub to remove any lichen or grime is all that is required in the way of upkeep.

◁ Steamer chairs look equally at home in an informal cottage-style garden or on the stone flags of a more minimalist design. This handsome pair make an elegant addition to a beautifully paved patio with its richly coloured slate and stone surface.

Al fresco eating

For most people, at least half the benefit of a city garden is the opportunity to eat and drink out of doors when the weather permits. Once a purely Mediterranean concept, outdoor eating has spread into more temperate climates, with the addition of some all-weather screening from the worst of the elements.

The scale and style of your entertaining out of doors will obviously depend on the space you have available, but for many people a barbecue is a must for the summer months. Such a large range are now manufactured that you are almost certainly spoiled for choice, and you can have anything from

a good old-fashioned scouts' barbecue – a couple of twigs and a pole over an open fire – to a mini-oven, powered with bottled gas.

If you are going to cook out of doors, you should think about it carefully. First of all, it is important to consider all the safety aspects. Do not site the barbecue too close to buildings or fences, or plants, particularly precious ones that may suffer from scorch. Think about where the prevailing winds blow from, and do not organize your barbecue so that smoke drifts downwind over your guests. You should also try to ensure that smoke does not drift into the windows of neighbouring flats or houses. Although

it involves more fetching and carrying, a spot away from your house, and your neighbours, would be much wiser.

Some people prefer to build a permanent barbecue area out of bricks at a specific point in the garden, and this is probably very sensible if you have the room to do so. Make sure, however, that you have taken the preceding points into account when planning where to site it.

Finally, make sure you have some kind of permanent table or sturdy trolley you can use while cooking, keep a fireblanket close by, and keep any flammable or poisonous chemicals out of reach of children and away from naked flames.

Ornaments and statuary

The city garden is the ideal place to display garden ornaments. In a limited space, any ornament will immediately have a far greater effect, and you can use statues, containers, mirrors, sundials or whatever takes your fancy, and suits the style of the garden, to add interest to the garden design.

Containers

Containers are, without doubt, among the most versatile of garden ornaments, and do not necessarily have to be planted up, although you will probably wish to do so in particular situations.

A wide range of handsome large containers, in terracotta, lead or stone, is available, and can be used as a focal

◁ Ceramics and terracotta make an attractive addition to this sunny garden, creating a splash of colour. Yuccas, cordylines and agaves make an excellent planting choice.

point in any design, if chosen carefully. The main point to bear in mind is to keep the concept fairly simple, and not to mix materials too freely. If you like terracotta, it is best to stick to this as a unifying theme. There are some wonderful imported large terracotta pots, handsome enough to stand as sculptural objects in their own right, if they are positioned carefully.

▷ Siting a statue at the end of a walkway or alley will help to create a focal point, and acts as a frame for the ornament. Planting the pergola with wisteria, roses and clematis, softens the structure while providing colour throughout the summer months. The space under it makes an ideal eating or relaxing area on hot days.

Sculpture

Sculptures in a range of styles and forms can enhance the garden too. You can choose special pieces at garden sculpture galleries or visit artists direct to commission your own. A sculptor will usually specialize in a particular material, be it ceramics, stone, bronze, clay or wood, and your choice will be determined by your own taste. Texture plays an important part in any sculptural piece, and you may be more attracted to the natural warmth of wood than to the cool surface of granite, for example. Again, you need to choose a material that works well with the others in your garden; colours and textures should combine harmoniously.

If you have just a little money and are wondering what you can afford, it pays to buy one good, notable piece than to dissipate your cash on several small ones. The garden setting demands a reasonably dramatic, theatrical concept, and a large piece will return your investment with dividends by being noticed and appreciated by garden visitors. Lots of small sculptures may simply jostle for attention.

It is important when siting a good piece of sculpture to find a situation which shows it off to advantage, and possibly one where it can be lit in the evening for maximum effect. Small

busts can be sited on plinths or set against a wall for example, surrounded by appropriate planting – ideally attractive foliage plants that form a soft frame; ivy, for example, is ideal.

Other ornaments

Architectural relics of various types, including broken pieces of pilaster or coping stones, make good garden ornaments. Try to treat them sympathetically and incorporate them into a design that bears some echo of their original style – be it classical, Gothic or post modern.

Cisterns, water tanks, and even old sinks can be converted to garden use. If

handsome enough, they can stand alone, or they can be planted sympathetically or converted into useful water features.

Mirrors can be used to great effect in small gardens to increase the apparent space by reflecting views. This approach works very well in small basements, where a mirror will not only increase the available space but will also help to reflect light. You need to be a little careful where and how you site mirrors, since the angle is important. One way it is often done is to surround the mirror with a trellis arch, thereby creating a 'trompe l'oeil' effect of a doorway into another part of the garden.

Lighting

▷ Subtly positioned, uplighters can create rich shadows, outlining features and creating a sense of drama in the garden – only a few such lights are needed. Organize the electrical plan carefully to provide the best position for the lights on one circuit.

If you are going to spend time and energy creating a city garden, it is well worthwhile expending a little more time and money lighting it. Lighting the garden has many benefits, not all immediately obvious. In any town garden, it is a boon for security. Very few burglars will walk through a lit garden to start fiddling with windows or locks, and it also gives you a good view from indoors.

Lighting the garden will also mean that you can enjoy the grandeur of your garden at night as well as in the daytime. Just a couple of judiciously placed lights can give your garden some of the dramatic appeal of a stage set. Trees and shrubs take on wonderful new outlines, the contrasts in light and shade enhancing their qualities and character enormously. If you want to use the garden for entertaining, then lights are a must, allowing you to extend your opportunities to do so into the evenings. Make sure the seating area is well, but subtly lit, the lights facing away from the area, not glaring onto it.

Choosing lighting

Lighting schemes do not have to be elaborate or expensive. At their simplest, they can take the form of a few flares on supports. Flares – rather like candles on stilts – are available from most garden centres and will burn for about six to eight hours, depending on size. They cast a beautifully soft warm glow and look extremely romantic.

A simple lighting system might incorporate two or three all–weather lights, fixed to spikes secured in the

◁ Lighting does not need to be a major outlay. A few candles in holders, judiciously positioned, can transform the atmopshere of the garden at night. Flares are also good and will burn for four to five hours. They provide an effective deterrent to flying insects as well!

▽ More ambitious lighting
schemes can turn your garden
into an outdoor room – a true
extension of the house. This
courtyard blends seamlessly
with the living space.

ground and angled to create a spot of
light wherever it seems most suitable or
convenient. One light, for example,
could be a downlighter onto the seating
area, and two more could be fixed at
further points in the garden to focus on
specific features – a water feature,
perhaps, or a particularly attractive
shrub or tree.

If you are using your patio for
entertaining, then make sure that you
also install any necessary lights for
safety of access as well – for example,
lighting the way along a path or down
steps. The aim is to sit bathed in a subtle
light, not the full glare of a floodlit
football pitch, so direct the light
upwards or downwards as required,
away from any seating.

If you have an attractive water feature,
you can light it using waterproof
underwater lights, which can enhance
its appeal greatly. If you can afford to,
make sure some of the lights are on
separate circuits so that you can switch
different lights on or off, as required.

Lights suitable for outdoor use are
generally available in the three
following types: tungsten lights, which
create a warm, golden glow; discharge
sodium or mercury lights, which give a
diffused slightly greenish tinged glow;
and low-voltage halogen lights, which
give a very white light.

PLANTING THE CITY GARDEN

C HOOSING THE APPROPRIATE plants for the setting and situation taxes even experienced gardeners. In this chapter, the different kinds of setting that determine the range of plants you can successfully grow are examined, from sunny dry patios to damp shady parts of the garden. In additional, special plants are needed for particular purposes – for screening, for creating a focal point, or for providing a few delicious fruits or vegetables – and this section offers a range of choices, plus useful planting lists. It is important too, when space is limited, to choose the plants that offer the most value – ideally with more than one season of interest.

◁ Pelargoniums are deservedly popular for city gardens. They flower for a long season, require almost no maintenance and look terrific, particularly in a single colour theme.

▷ Foliage has its part to play as well as flowers, as this shady patio with its topiary, beautiful ancient fig tree, trained standards and tree fern demonstrates.

Planting the city garden

Choosing appropriate plants for a city garden is an amalgam of common sense and imagination. It is important to make some practical choices, because of the constraints of small spaces, often difficult planting conditions and the need to choose plants that offer the best value. The element of imagination is equally important, as the planting will bring the garden to life.

To get the most from a small space, it pays to have a clear planting theme in your mind's eye, to appreciate the limitations of the conditions – shade, sun, damp ground and so on – and then to try to unify the planting. But, to the uninititated, what does this mean? For a start, it probably means having a balance of vertical interest – climbers, larger shrubs and even the odd tree – and horizontal interest – smaller shrubs, perennials, bulbs and annuals. You do not, in fact, need a wide variety of different plants to make a garden look well planted, but their position in the garden is crucial.

Not everyone grasps that big plants can do very well in small spaces. As a consequence, they tend to choose lots of smaller plants, which will not only give the garden a bitty, restless look, but which are much more labour intensive. Among the big bold plants that would do well in a city garden are evergreen shrubs, such as the broad-leaved *Fatsia*

◁ A study in green, white and silver, this small urn, filled with *Helichrysum petiolaris* and surrounded by thickly ribbed hosta leaves and clipped box, makes a perfect planting scheme for a small shady corner.

japonica and the yellow-splashed *Aucuba japonica* 'Crotonifolia', spiky cordylines and yuccas and the attractive *Choisya ternata*, with its whorl-like leaves and clouds of scented white flowers in early summer.

It is important to ensure that the garden has some kind of structural frame of planting, around which smaller groups of plants, including perennials and annuals, can be composed. Even if you have no more than a balcony or terrace, it is still worth including a couple of evergreen shrubs – maybe in the form of twinned containers of topiary shaps of box or myrtle – to provide a peg on which to hang the remainder of the planting.

If you cannot afford, in the first year of the garden, to plant it up extensively, then concentrate your planting efforts and, if you can, buy the bigger elements first, perhaps filling in the empty spaces with big annuals that you grow yourself from seed – tobacco plants are excellent space fillers and do well in partial shade as well as sun, unlike many of the annuals. In the first summer, take any cuttings you can and make sure you do this each year to increase your stock of shrubs. Quite a few perennials can be layered or divided to augment supplies.

It is often best to pick several species from one genus that you know will

◁ Pairs of containers, whether of architectural plants, such as these topiary box spirals, or of flowering plants, such as standard marguerites or fuchsias, are ideal for creating emphasis in the garden, for instance to mark a doorway, as here. Try to ensure that the scale of the planted containers suits the setting.

work well in the environment than to go for a range of different plants. Planting gains its impact from making a bold statement, and grouping plants by type certainly increases the effect. Pelargoniums are a must for any city garden, not least because of the many different forms, which include trailing types for hanging baskets, richly scented ivy-leaved ones that can be used in cooking, and brilliant-coloured flowering regal and zonal pelargoniums, some of which can even be trained into architectural standards. Fuchsias are another good candidate, again with a wide range of flower types and colours. Like pelargoniums, they can be trained into standards, if you wish.

It is well worth considering the seasonal element of the planting, and doing your best to ensure that the garden offers year-round interest. This is obviously harder to do in very small spaces, but even on a window sill you can change the planting as the seasons progress, so that you always have something interesting to observe. A windowbox could house spring bulbs, followed by a selection of summer flowers and herbs, with late-summer annuals and chrysanthemums for autumn, and heathers, cyclamens and ivies in winter, for example.

Plants for screening

▷ If you have a pergola, roses are the ideal companion for it, possibly with other climbing plants, such as clematis or honeysuckle, climbing over and among them to provide a longer flowering season.

One of the most essential requirements of a city garden is to provide privacy from neighbouring flats and houses and screening from cold winds and pollution, or, for that matter, from marauding cats. You may also want to obscure an unattractive view.

In classic garden designs, screening is usually provided by formal clipped evergreens, which are dense and impenetrable – yews and hollies, for example, make excellent dark solid screens. However, both are fairly slow growing, and you may well need plants that will do their work faster, unless you plan to stay in your city apartment or house for some time to come.

CLIMBERS

Abutilon megapotamicum
Akebia quinata
Aristolochia macrophylla
Campsis x *tagliabuana*
Clematis armandii
C. macropetala
C. montana
C. tangutica
Eccremocarpus scaber (annual)
Hedera (many varieties)
Humulus lupulus 'Aureus'
Hydrangea anomala petiolaris
Jasminum officinale
Ipomoea tricolor (annual)
Lathyrus latifolius
Lonicera periclymenum
L. x *tellmanniana*
Passiflora caerulea
Rosa (many varieties)
Solanum crispum 'Glasnevin'
Trachelospermum jasminoides
Tropaeolum speciosum (perennial)
Vitis vinifera 'Purpurea'
Wisteria sinensis

◁ Trellis, over which you can grow climbers, such as this handsome ivy, *Hedera canariensis* 'Gloire de Marengo', makes an excellent screen for a small town garden and an attractive backdrop for this pair of architetural plants trained as standards.

Climbing plants

For faster cover, climbing plants trained over tall trellis are a better option. There is a wide choice of suitable plants, some offering much more dense cover than others. Ivies are excellent value as they are fairly quick growing – you will get a couple of metres in two or three years out of some of the swifter growing varieties – and so are the creepers, some of which you might find a little too enthusiastic, however. Parthenocissus can put on many feet in one season, but it dies back in winter, unlike ivy, so it will provide a screen only in the summer months.

Tall bamboos are an excellent choice for cover up to about 3m (10ft) in height, but you may be best advised to plant them in containers. Bamboos spread by underground rhizomes and your whole garden may well turn into a bamboo thicket unless you control their spread in some way. If you do grow them in containers, you will need to root prune them every couple of years. One solution is to grow them in a plastic container within a larger terracotta one. Every couple of years, you can dismantle the plastic container, trim out the roots (up to one third) and then replant it into a similar-sized pot (see page 117).

One of the nicest screening plants is a vine – either a fruiting sort or a strictly ornamental one. The leaves are large and attractive, and turn a pretty russet colour in autumn before they fall. Another good screening plant is Dutchman's Pipe (*Aristolochia*

WALL SHRUBS

Acca sellowiana (evergreen)
Ceanothus 'Burkwoodii' (evergreen)
Chaenomeles speciosa
Choisya ternata (evergreen)
Cotoneaster horizontalis
Crinodendron hookerianum
  (evergreen)
Escallonia 'Apple Blossom'
(evergreen)
Euonymus fortunei (evergreen)
Forsythia suspensa
Fremontodendron 'California Glory'
Garrya elliptica (evergreen)
Magnolia grandiflora (evergreen)
Myrtus communis (evergreen)
Pittosporum tenuifolium (evergreen)

▷ This singularly beautiful formal foliage garden demonstrates just how successful a garden can be without the benefit of flowers; here the varying shapes and forms provide an almost sculptural feel to the garden. Compartmentalizing the garden, by screening the view with evergreens, as here, helps to enlarge the apparent space, as the eye cannot take in all the areas of the garden in one go.

PLANTS FOR A QUICK SCREEN

Chamaecyparis lawsoniana
Cotoneaster x *watereri*
Eucalyptus gunnii
Fallopia baldschuanica
Hedera helix
Ligustrum japonicum
L. lucidum
Pleioblastus
Pyracantha
Sorbus aria
S. aucuparia
Thuja plicata

FLOWERING SMALL TREES

Cercis siliquastrum
Cornus controversa
Crataegus laevigata
Hamamelis mollis
Laburnum
Magnolia salicifolia
M. x *soulangeana*
Malus x *schiedeckeri*
Prunus serrulata
P. subhirtella
Robinia kelseyi
Syringa vulgaris

EVERGREEN TREES

Arbutus x *andrachnoides*
A. menziesii
Ceanothus arboreus
Chamaecyparis lawsoniana
Elaeagnus x *ebbingei*
Eucalyptus gunnii
Ilex aquifolium
Laurus nobilis
Magnolia grandiflora
Nothofagus menziesii
Quercus coccifera
Taxus baccata
Umbellularia californica

macrophylla), which has vine-like leaves and can be trained along poles or wires to form an attractive ribbon shape at the top of a fence, for example. Equally good is the golden hop (*Humulus lupulus* 'Aureus').

There is nothing to stop you using flowering climbers for screening purposes, and roses can make the best screens against cats, their thorny branches forming an impenetrable thicket, while offering the bonus of a once (or twice if you pick a remontant rose) a year glorious display of flowers, most with delicious scent as well. 'New Dawn' seems universally popular and does well in most situations, its pale pink flowers blending well with most colour schemes. Another tough and vigorous contender is the richly scented, bright pink 'Albertine', or you could try one of the really big varieties, such as *Rosa filipes* 'Kiftsgate' if you have enough space for it to stretch itself – it will climb to 9m (30ft) or more, covering itself in clouds of white flowers in summer.

Trees as screens
If you have an unsightly view to screen, a tall columnar tree – *Chamaecyparis lawsoniana*, for example – does the trick most effectively. Plant it as close to the house as you dare without doing damage to the foundations (say 45m/15ft away). Another good screening tree is *Eucalyptus gunnii*, which will survive furious pruning to twist and turn towards the light. The leaves on the adult tree are long, light and feathery, and although few would recommend it for a small garden, it should do very well in a garden of, say, 12m (40ft) or more in length. Silver birches are also good for screening with dappled light and shade, as is the delicate winter flowering cherry, *Prunus subhirtella* 'Autumnalis'.

Plants for focal points

▷ This brilliantly coloured planting scheme for a hot, sunny corner of the garden makes a strong statement with a variegated-leaved *Phormium*, deep red lupins and bright orange calendulas in the foreground.

When planning a small garden you need to ensure that the eye is drawn to specific elements in it, rather than allowed to meander over it in an apparently random way. In larger gardens, designers normally create a series of compartments which help to focus attention on individual elements within the larger whole. In a small garden, this luxury is not really applicable, as the space will not normally allow it, although you can copy the concept by giving different parts of the garden a specific theme, or by creating points of interest with garden ornaments or particular plants.

The plants that serve this kind of purpose best are those with strong architectural interest, simply because you need something reasonably large to catch the eye. Ideally, such as plant should look good most of the year, becoming a more or less permanent feature of the garden. You can, of course, use perennials or deciduous shrubs for the same purpose, but you will want to ensure that the garden landscape still looks good without them in the winter months.

Architectural shrubs

Among the best shrubs to act as a focal point are those with distinctive foliage and a handsome form. A good subject is *Fatsia japonica,* an evergreen with large glossy divided leaves and attractive berries in winter. It forms a pretty large bush eventually, and can make a good end of border plant to screen the end of the garden from the house. Another good candidate is the Mexican orange blossom, *Choisya ternata,* or the winter-flowering *Mahonia* x *media* 'Charity'; both have the benefit of being scented, too, although not everyone likes the rather foxy perfume of the Mexican orange blossom. Equally good for this purpose would be large spiky leaved cordylines or yuccas, perhaps in a container, or the Abyssinian banana plant, *Ensete ventricosum,* again in a container, as you will need to overwinter it indoors. A large palm, such as *Trachycarpus fortunei* or the tree fern, *Dicksonia antarctica,* makes a good focal point for a paved or gravel surface.

Using arches

If you do not want the plant in a solo spot, then consider creating an arch, over which you can grow a few climbers or twining plants. This, again, will draw the eye, particularly in summer when plants are in flower, though of course you could, if you prefer, turn it into a permanent feature by planting evergreen climbers, such as ivies, over it. Alternatively, use it as a support for some exotic-looking foliage climbers, such as big-leaved vines, the evergreen clematis, *Clematis armandii,* which is also scented, or the climbing hydrangea, *Hydrangea anomala petiolaris,* with its large flat corymbs of creamy flowers. In warmer areas, you could try *Campsis* x *tagliabuana* 'Madame Galen' with its wonderful burnt-orange trumpet-shaped flowers.

SHRUBS AND TREES

Acer palmatum dissectum
  'Atropurpureum'
Brugmansia (tender)
Buxus sempervirens (as topiary)
Camellia
Catalpa speciosa (trained as
  standard)
Dicksonia antarctica
Ensete ventricosum (tender)
Fatsia japonica
x *Fatshedera lizei*
Fuchsia (trained as standard)
Hydrangea
Lonicera (trained as standard)
Magnolia x *soulangeana*
Rhododendron yakushimanum
Taxus baccata (as topiary)
Trachycarpus fortunei

LARGE FLOWERING
PERENNIALS AND
BULBS

Allium christophii
Camassia leichtlinii
Campanula latifolia
Canna (flowers)
Cardiocrinum giganteum (flowers)
Cosmos bipinnatus (flowers)
Crambe cordifolia (flowers and
  foliage)
Crocosmia 'Lucifer'
Delphinium
Digitalis purpurea
Hemerocallis
Heracleum mantegazzianum
  (foliage and flowers – poisonous)
Ligularia dentata 'Desdemona'
  (flowers and foliage)
Lilium hybrids
Lobelia cardinalis
Nicotiana sylvestris (flowers)
Verbascum olympicum (flowers)

Perennials

A small bed of large perennials can also provide a focal point. Try creating a bed with some show-stopping perennials that grow to 1.2m (4ft) or more – *Euphorbia characias wulfenii*, ligularias, rodgersias and the big hellebore, *Helleborus argutifolias*, are all good candidates for this kind of treatment, with perhaps some smaller perennials edging the bed and sprawling over the neighbouring paving – try the small campanulas, epimediums and geraniums for this purpose.

To create interest at the furthest point of the garden, use some really big perennials. Clouds of *Crambe cordifolia*, with its big blue-green leaves and starry white flowers, and some silver-leaved giants, such as *Erygnium giganteum*,

would be good for a fairly sunny spot, while *Macleaya cordata* would combine well with *Crocosmia* 'Lucifer' in a slightly less sunny situation.

Plants in containers

A big container with a handsome architectural plant, such as *Hosta sieboldiana elegans* or a white-flowered hydrangea, could provide a punctuation point where two different kinds of surface meet. In a formal, oriental-style design, you could use single specimens of mound-forming shrubs to create a similar full-stop. Yakushimanum rhododendrons, a neat *Skimmia japonica* or *Viburnum davidii* will all make handsome, fairly low mounds, or you can clip plants, such as box or privet, into ball shapes.

FOLIAGE
PERENNIALS

Angelica archangelica
Arundo donax
Astilboides tabularis
Bergenia cordifolia
Cordyline australis
Cynara cardunculus
Darmera peltata
Gunnera manicata
Hosta sieboldiana elegans
Macleaya cordata
Miscanthus sinensis 'Zebrinus'
Petasites japonicus giganteus
Rheum palmatum
Yucca gloriosa
Zantedeschia aethiopica

Plants for containers

Containers are a must for most city gardens. Not only do they allow you to grow plants in inhospitable places, including high-rise roof gardens and balconies, but they also give you a great deal of flexibility, as you can move them about. This is imperative in a small space, where you need to get the most from your plants – moving a container into pride of place as the plants within it come into flower is an essential aspect of city gardening.

The choice of plants for containers is vast, and you need to get away from the traditional container plants concepts, which tend to focus too much on hanging baskets and floral displays and too little on the handsome architectural foliage plants, which have a very strong role to play in the city garden.

Foliage plants

One of the greatest contenders for a container is the hosta (or plantain lily as it used to be commonly known). There are many different forms, but one of the large varieties, with huge, thickly ribbed bluish green waxy leaves,

FOLIAGE PLANTS

Acer palmatum dissectum
Brassica oleracea 'Sekito'
Buxus sempervirens
Chamaecyparis nootkatensis
  'Pendula'
Clivia miniata
Corydalis lutea
Dicksonia antarctica
Euphorbia characias wulfenii
Hedera helix
Heuchera 'Palace Purple'
Hosta fortunei
H. sieboldiana
Juniperus scopulorum
Milium effusum
Ensete ventricosum
Myrtus communis
Zantedeschia aethiopica

◁ Foliage plants can create as much impact in containers as flowering plants. Here the contrasting forms of hostas with their broadly ribbed leaves, and ground elder, in a pretty variegated form, make an attractive display by a doorway. Make sure that any foliage plants are in attractive terracotta or ceramic pots.

▷ A little stepped area provides a home for a number of herbs, among them a bay (*Laurus nobilis*) trained as a standard, lavender, viola and roses. Containers are invaluable for adding interest at different heights, and can be moved around as the plants come in and out of flower.

makes a wonderful rosette shape in a container – a handsome sight even when out of flower. In flower it produces a tall, white spire of lily-like flowers. Hostas planted in beds are prey to slug damage, but planting them in containers helps to reduce this problem, particularly if you set the container on a bed of sharp grit. Several different forms planted together make an excellent display from May until the leaves turn in autumn.

FLOWERING TREES AND SHRUBS

Abutilon megapotamicum (wall shrub)
Actinidia kolomikta (climber)
Brugmansia x *candida*
Camellia japonica
Cobaea scandens (climber)
Fuchsia 'Leonora'
F. 'Thalia'
Hibiscus rosa-sinensis
Hydrangea macrophylla
Magnolia stellata
M. x *soulangeana*
Nerium oleander
Passiflora caerulea (climber)
Rhododendron yakushimanum
Rosa (climbers and shrubs)

There are plenty of other foliage plants to choose from for containers. One worthwhile solution is to pick a fairly small or slow-growing evergreen, plant it in the centre of the container, and change the planting around it from season to season. A clipped box ball in the centre of a medium-sized pot can play host to snowdrops or small white tulips in spring and glistening white osteospermums ('Whirlygig' is particularly striking) in summer, followed by button chrysanthemums or cyclamens in autumn . A few ivy plants to trail over the side helps to break the formality of the pot.

Even trees can be grown in large pots, and one of the best performers in this respect is the Japanese maple (*Acer palmatum*) with its delicate, hand-shaped filigree leaves. Some of them turn brilliant colours in autumn, and although expensive, are well worth including in a city garden. Be warned, however, that some are sensitive to wind chill and may not survive in an exposed position unless given additional shelter.

Flowering plants
In spring you can create massed displays of bulbs, ideally with some kind of orchestrated colour theme, be it a single colour or a twinned theme, such as yellow and blue, for example. If you plant a good number of tulips or hyacinths together in a pot, they look far more impressive than scattered amongst other bulbs.

In summer you can create a mini border effect by putting containers of larger annuals and perennials behind the smaller ones. Big tobacco plants,

△ Displaying containers in small spaces can be solved by using vertical as well as horizontal space, as this neatly tiered stand, with its pots of matching pansies, demonstrates very effectively.

lilies, or alliums, with perhaps achillea or cosmos, could form the back row, while smaller plants – daisies, helianthemums, pelargoniums and so on – form the front rank. Again, it helps to have some kind of colour scheme, but it can be either softly toning – blues, pinks, whites and silvers, perhaps – or a strong strident contrast of hot colours – yellows, pinks and reds, for example –

FLOWERING BULBS,
ANNUALS AND
PERENNIALS

Agapanthus africanus
Allium christophii
Anemone x *hybrida*
Begonia
Brachycome iberidifolia
Canna indica
Chrysanthemum
Clivia miniata
Dahlia
Dicentra spectabilis
Helleborus
Impatiens
Lantana camara
Lewisia
Lilium 'Regale'
Lobelia
Muscari armeniacum
Narcissus
Osteospermum
Pelargonium (many forms)
Penstemon 'Andenken an Friedrich
    Hahn'
Petunia
Primula
Salvia sclarea turkestanica
Silene
Tulipa
Viola

depending on the style of the garden and the situation.

If you want to grow larger climbers, you will need to ensure that they have a large enough pot in which to spread their roots, but most climbers can be successfully grown in a pot about 45cm (18in) in diameter. The plants will, of course, need to be watered regularly, and fed during the growing season, as the container will limit their ability to take up food and water through the normal processes, and it will be up to you to supply it for them.

The ubiquitous pelargonium often forms the centrepiece of a flowering display in summer. There are many different forms to choose from, with attractively marked leaves as well as different shapes and colours of flower, and it is worth while going to a specialist pelargonium nursery to pick out some of the more interesting forms. Those such as *P. graveolens*, with its deliciously fragrant pale green leaves and bushy habit, make excellent container plants and a good foil for some of the more brightly coloured flowering ones. They grow so easily, in the main, from cuttings that you can quickly increase your stock of them.

The new breeds of busy lizzie, the New Guinea hybrids, are also worth looking out for. Although more

◁ Here, too, vertical space has been well used for a mixed display of flowering plants in containers, in shades of pink – asters, salvia, busy lizzies and ornamental cabbages among them. Keeping to a single or toning colour scheme will help increase the feeling of space.

expensive than the usual types, their form, their leaf colour and shape, and their flowers are infinitely more striking. They do, however, need copious and frequent watering, and, unlike pelargoniums, will wilt and die rapidly if neglected, but they are an excellent choice for a shady alley, as they thrive in partially shaded conditions.

Wall pots and hanging baskets

If attractively planted, wall pots and hanging baskets can transform a high-walled patio or semi-basement, and there is nothing to stop you using shade-loving plants, if the situation demands it. Ferns and ferny leaved plants, such as corydalis, work well in these kinds of settings. So do the delicate trailing plants like verbenas and diascia, wandering sailor (*Tradescantia*) and nasturtiums, although these all benefit from a sunnier situation. Pansies are good candidates for hanging baskets, as are begonias and lobelia, and of course trailing helichrysum and nepeta. You will get a more attractive effect if you limit the planting to three or four different plants in one container, and opt for a limited colour palette – a couple of toning colours – rather than the archetypal blaze of colour previously associated with hanging baskets.

Water-loving plants

▷ For poolside plantings, in damp ground, the arum lily (*Zantedeschia aethiopica*) with its handsome white flower spathes and large green leaves, and hostas (with their thickly ribbed leaves, in the foreground) are ideal companions. For colour in this situation, candlestick primulas, in big drifts, are ideal.

Some plants thrive in deep water, some in shallow water and some simply in moist soil. If you have a small garden, you can, without too much difficulty, make a small pond or water feature, which will have the double bonus not only of creating additional visual interest, but also of increasing your choice of plants to grow. If you make the pond using a butyl liner, you could also create a bog garden alongside the pool. This will add an even greater variety to your plant list, and will make the pond look infinitely more natural, as in the wild, ponds are sited in marshy soil and their surrounds are populated with damp-loving plants. (The single greatest, but commonly made, mistake in water gardening is to site a pond in a desert-like area of the garden – the two simply do not work together and will never look right.)

Bog and marginal plants

If you want to dispense with a pond and just opt for a bog garden, there is still a wide range of plants that like wet conditions that you can grow. The big handsome ornamental rhubarb, *Rheum palmatum*, is happy with its feet in damp soil, provided it is fed well. Ligularias and rodgersias will thrive, as will some of the hostas and the big semi-evergreen geranium, *Geranium palmatum*. Also happy in these conditions are feathery looking astilbes, the sinister (and poisonous) monkshood, *Aconitum*, and striking drumstick primulas, with their raised heads of brightly coloured flowers. These latter look best planted in quite large drifts, rather than scattered among other plants.

Grasses look particularly good and some favour damp conditions and so are ideally suited to the bog garden.

◁ Among the most beautiful water-loving plants is *Iris laevigata* which comes in both purple and yellow forms. This one is *I.l.*'Atropurpurea'. Damp-loving plants tend to grow generously, in large clumps, and it is important that poolside planting echoes this feature.

DAMP-LOVING PLANTS

Artemisia lactiflora
Astilbe x *arendsii*
Astilboides tabularis
Eupatorium purpureum
Filipendula palmata
Hosta fortunei
H. sieboldiana
Iris ensata
I. laevigata
I. sibirica
Lysimachia nummularia
Lythrum salicaria
Persicaria bistorta 'Superba'
Primula florindae
P. japonica
Rheum palmatum
Trollius europaeus

Among the best are *Miscanthus sinensis* 'Zebrinus', with gold-striped leaves, and *Carex alata* 'Aurea', which also has golden foliage.

For growing in shallow water, again some irises are ideal, in particular the Japanese irises, such as *Iris ensata* or *I. laevigata*. These have not only particularly pretty flowers, in delicate shades of blue, mauve, white or yellow, but also handsome evergreen sword-shaped leaves. Equally good for shallow

REEDS, RUSHES
AND GRASSES

Acorus calamus 'Variegatus'
Arundo donax
Carex alata 'Aurea'
Cyperus alternifolius
Miscanthus sinensis 'Zebrinus'
Phalaris arundinacea
Scirpus tabernaemontani 'Zebrinus'

water are marsh marigolds (*Caltha palustris*) and the pickerel weed, with its glossy dark green leaves and spikes of bright blue flowers.

Floating plants

If your pond is at least lm (3ft) deep, you can grow singularly beautiful water lilies, which come in a range of colours. The smallest is Nymphae tetragona (the dwarf water lily), which is suitable for most small garden ponds with a depth of up to 30cm (12in). It comes in several colours, but the common white form is one of the most attractive. Another good deep-water pond plant is the water hawthorn (*Aponogeton distachyos*), which will cope with a shadier site than will the water lily. Its leaves, which are elongated and rather elegant, float in the same manner as those of a water lily, and it has waxy spires of flowers that lie horizontally above the surface of the water for a long flowering season.

Oxygenating plants

If you aim to keep fish in your pond, you will need to have oxygenating plants (which will also benefit any pond, as they help to keep the water fresh). There is a wide range to choose from, but some of the most commonly used are *Elodea canadensis* (Canadian pondweed) and *Potamogeton crispus* (curled pondweed). The water violet, *Hottonia palustris*, is one of the prettiest oxygenating plants, with ferny leaves and pale mauve flowers that rise above the water.

FLOATING AND
OXYGENATING
PLANTS

Aponogeton distachyos
Eichhornia crassipes
Elodea canadensis
Hottonia palustris
Hydrocharis morsus-ranae
Nuphar lutea
Nymphaea alba
N. 'Escarboule'
N. tetragona
Orontium aquaticum
Potamegoton crispus
Ranunculus aquatilis
Trapa natans

Plants for shade

▽ Among other good shade-loving plants, grouped here around the bole of a tree in the corner of a garden, are ligularias. Two forms, *L. dentata* 'Desdemona' and *L. tangutica* 'The Rocket', both have handsome large leaves and striking golden or orange flowers in summer.

Although there are only a very few plants that will cope with deep shade – most notably ivies – most gardens have at least some light, and there is a much wider variety that will cope with these partially shaded conditions. Some prefer the shade to be dry and others cope better in damp soil, but provided you take the time and trouble to find out which plants will thrive, you can create wonderful gardens in relatively inauspicious conditions.

If you want privacy in your garden, and plant trees or large shrubs to provide it, the areas beneath their canopy are already earmarked for shade-loving small shrubs and

SMALL PLANTS FOR SHADE

Alchemilla mollis
Corydalis lutea
Epimedium grandiflorum
Geranium macrorrhizum
G. phaeum
Hedera helix (climber)
Hepatica
Impatiens New Guinea hybrids
Pulmonaria longiifolia
Symphytum ibericum

perennials. Indeed, it is well worth your while, even in a tiny garden, having at least one large shrub or small tree, just so that you can vary the habitat provided, and increase the range of plants you can grow.

In a small garden, you are unlikely to get too much damp shade, unless you live in a part of the country with very high rainfall. The shade cast by buildings in cities, let alone any trees, is more than likely to create dry soil

▷ Hostas, ferns, bamboos and ornamental maples are all good subjects for partially shaded patio gardens, seen here attractively interplanted among large York stone slabs and gravel in an Oriental-style garden setting.

conditions as well, so it is these drier shady conditions that you will, in the main, have to contend with. Bear in mind that the area under the canopy of a tree receives relatively little rain, so this shade will be drier than most.

Fortunately, there are some very attractive plants at your disposal, although you may need to rethink some of your gardening concepts. Brightly coloured displays of hot coloured annuals will not be for you. In their place, you can grow some singularly beautiful foliage plants and a few flowering ones that cope with these conditions, although their flowers tend

MEDIUM PLANTS FOR SHADE

Acanthus mollis
Aconitum (poisonous)
Asplenium scolopendrium
Digitalis purpurea
Dryopteris filix-mas
Euphorbia
Helleborus argutifolius
Hemerocallis
Polypodium vulgare
Polystichum setiferum
Rodgersia
Trachystemon orientalis

to be in paler shades – whites and pale blues predominating. A green and white garden – the result of this kind of planting – looks extremely good in most cityscapes, and is very restful and relaxing to the eye. Once you have got used to the concept, you will find your eye is more attuned to noticing shape, form and texture – all virtues of shade-loving plants.

Some of the plants that do well in this kind of situation have already cropped up in other parts of this book, most notably as architectural focal point contenders, since many of them have handsome form and attractive foliage. The ubiquitous hosta, is probably the

king of all shade-loving plants and should definitely be a major player in any shade planting scheme. Other larger shade-loving plants you could try include *Acanthus mollis*, big-leaved bergenias, foxgloves (*Digitalis*), hellebores, and Solomon's seal (*Polygonatum*).

Low-growing plants for shade include the bugle (*Ajuga*), little anemones and cyclamens, the deadnettle (*Lamium maculatum*), and the rather invasive evergreen *Vinca minor*, which has pretty blue flowers. Other good candidates are epimediums, with little heart-shaped leaves, and *Tiarella cordifolia*, with its spires of white flowers.

▽ Ligularia in its summer guise flanks the steps in a shady corner. It looks best planted in containers, or in large drifts, as here. It needs damp soil if it is to do well, but looks equally good in a container, provided you keep it well watered.

Plants for shady walls

To clothe shady walls, ivies are the obvious choice, although the yellow-splashed or silver-variegated types will revert to all-green leaf colouring if deprived of sunlight. Other good candidates are creepers and vines; *Clematis montana* and *C. alpina* will both cope with a north-facing, shady wall. *Euonymus fortunei* can be grown as a wall shrub against a shady wall, as can *Garrya elliptica*. *Cotoneaster horizontalis*, *Crinodendron hookerianum*, *Humulus lupulus* 'Aureus' and *Lathyrus latifolius*, the everlasting pea, will all cope with partial shade, and *Passiflora caerulea*, normally supposed to like sun, can also

▷ Some of the more exotic plants, among them tree ferns and daturas, will cope well in semi-shaded conditions in mild climates, as this little group demonstrates. When grouping together plants in containers, try to get a good mixture of foliage types and sizes, to give variety to the planting when the flowers are no longer in season.

do quite well in an alleyway, although it will not grow as large or flower as freely here as in full sun.

At the foot of the wall, the shadiest part, ferns are ideal candidates, and look particularly good when planted in a ribbon formation alongside the wall. *Helleborus argutifolius*, the big evergreen hellebore with greenish flowers, copes well with partial shade, as do several of the euphorbias. Another good bet for this kind of situation is the big *Geranium phaeum*, a large evergreen with handsomely divided leaves.

Woodland plants

For a more woodland-style shade garden, consider growing some of the plants that do well in these conditions. Pulmonarias are among the most attractive shade-loving plants, and their attractively mottled leaves and pinkish purple bell-like flowers look particularly good when they are planted in large drifts. The scented lily-of-the-valley is another good contender for shade under trees, as are the hardy cyclamens, again with pretty white-splashed leaves. In the right conditions, both will rapidly spread to provide excellent ground cover.

There are a number of clump-forming plants that do well in shade,

including the attractive bronze-leaved hepatica with spires of blue flowers, and Japanese anemones, with white or pink flowers. The feathery leaved corydalis is another good plant for dry shade.

It is always worth growing a few bulbs in a semi-woodland area; snowdrops and primroses, in particular, thrive in partially shaded conditions. Both will do well in grass around the bole of a tree. Some species of narcissus, which are more delicate than the big blowsy daffodils, will also do well in light shade, and, of course, bluebells thrive in peaty soil and partial shade. A good combination would be a couple of big evergreen *Helleborus argutifolius* underplanted with bluebells.

GROUND COVER
FOR SHADE

Ajuga reptans
Bergenia
Epimedium
Ferns (various)
Euonymus
Hedera helix
Lamium maculatum
Pachysandra terminalis
Soleirolia
Tellima grandiflora
Tiarella cordifolia
Tolmeia menziesii
Vinca minor

Plants for dry sun

There is a rich and varied selection of plants, many of them from the Mediterranean regions of Europe, that do best in dry sunny situations. These are ideal plants for a hot, sunny patio or roof garden, or even a south- or west-facing balcony. Because they are so well adapted to drought conditions in their natural habitat, such plants are relatively low maintenance, requiring little attention and doing surprisingly well in fairly poor soil. Many of them have attractively silvered leaves, and you can make this a theme of the planting if you wish, perhaps marrying them with some plants with variegated leaves.

Among the best plants for dry sunny conditions are the wormwoods (*Artemisia*), of which there are many different forms and sizes. *Convoluvus cneorum* is a pretty slightly tender plant with very attractive blue green foliage and white flowers with a prominent yellow eye. Pinks do particularly well in hot sun, and those with the strongest scent, such as 'Mrs Sinkins', are perennially popular. Potentillas also do well in sunny places, and there are many different forms to choose from, from

MEDIUM PLANTS FOR DRY SUN

Achillea
Agapanthus africanus
Anthemis punctata cupaniana
Alstroemeria hybrids
Centaurea
Crambe cordifolia
Crocosmia
Cynara cardunculus
Euphorbia
Gladiolus
Kniphofia
Lavandula
Linum
Papaver
Penstemon
Perovskia
Phlomis
Phygelius
Salvia sclarea turkestanica
Sisyrinchium striatum
Verbascum

◁ Succulents, such as the agaves and echeveria shown here, do well in hot sunny gravel gardens, along with smaller succulents, such as sedums and saxifrages and some of the Mediteranean herbs, including thyme and marjoram. The soil must be free-draining, however.

◁ The gravel around this small patio provides a home for a rich display of dry-loving plants, including catmint, lady's mantle, ornamental thistles and anchusa. Gravel gardens present a good opportunity to plant Mediterranean plants, which enjoy drought conditions, in a loose, cottage style design.

quite large shrubs to little mat-forming ground-covering ones.

Ruta graveolens is another good foliage plant – a herb in fact – with strongly aromatic divided blue-green foliage; 'Jackman's Blue' is one of the most popular forms. *Santolina chamaecyparis* is another aromatic herb with silvery foliage that makes a good border edging. You can clip it back each autumn to make a mini hedge. *Brachyglottis laxifolia* is another good silvery leaved shrub, but a bit bigger (about l.2m/4ft) and will make a good edging to a patio, sprawling attractively over the paving. Lavender, too, makes an excellent edging for a path or border, and can be clipped back to keep it to a more formal shape.

Of the bigger shrubs, buddleias thrive in light soil and dry conditions, and the pretty *B. alternifolia* 'Argentea' has attractive silvery leaves and lavender, scented flowers in early summer.

Plants for cracks and crevices

If your garden has a sunny patio area, you can use the cracks and crevices to plant a range of sun-loving small perennials, which will help to soften the look of the paving. The same principle can be applied to the tops of walls, or crevices in a dry stone wall. Stone troughs and shallow containers also make ideal homes for these kinds of small sun-loving plants.

Among the best plants for this kind of situation are small saxifrages and sedums, which thrive in very dry poor soil. They have large fleshy leaves that retain moisture well, and make an attractive carpet of leaves, studded, when the time comes, with flowers on taller stems. For planting in the cracks of paving stones, try the little and aptly named daisy-gone-crazy, or *Erigeron karvinskianus*, with its array of pink fading to white daisy flowers. Also good

for crevices and cracks are the little campanulas, which seed themselves happily almost anywhere, as indeed does the larger *Alchemilla mollis*, with its velvety green-grey leaves and lime-green flowers. Another good candidate is baby's tears (*Soleirolia soleirolii*).

SMALL PLANTS FOR CRACKS IN PAVING

Acaena
Achillea (dwarf forms)
Anemone fulgens
Armeria
Aubrieta
Aurinia
Dianthus
Diascia
Erigeron karvinskianus
Geranium (dwarf forms)
Helianthemum
Lewisia
Origanum
Oxalis
Potentilla (dwarf forms)
Raoulia
Sedum
Sempervivum
Silene
Thymus

Plants for wild gardens

These days, almost everyone has become ecology conscious, and although you may not want to turn your whole garden into a wildlife haven, it is well worth considering, even in a small city garden, consecrating one area of it to plants that help to keep birds, butterflies and some humbler insects supplied with food, or failing that, to have at least a few such plants in the garden.

It can come as a surprise to find out just how easy it is to grow plants that serve such a worthwhile function; in the main, they are plants that appear naturally in the landscape. The humble nettle, the food for many caterpillars, is pulled up by most gardeners on sight, yet is a worthy plant to allow to flourish, if only in a small patch by the compost bin.

One of the best ways to transform your garden into a more ecologically friendly environment is to do it in stages. If your garden has a traditional patch of lawn, with shrub borders around it, as many gardens do even in cities, why not plant some butterfly-attracting plants near the house in containers – thymes, lavenders, tobacco plants, geraniums and petunias? You could then plant some alyssum, thrift and small campanulas over any low walls you may have.

Wildflower meadows

If you have space, you could turn the lawn at the end of the garden into a mini wildflower meadow, letting the grass grow and planting in it a mixture of wild flowers and grasses. The grass here should be cut only twice a year, in mid and late summer. If the lawn is large enough, mow a section through it to provide an attractive pathway.

Among the wild flowers that thrive in grass are poppies (*Papaver rhoeas*), cornflowers (*Centaurea cyanus*), knapweed (*Centaurea nigra*), yarrow (*Achillea millefolium*) and ox-eye daisies (*Leucanthemum vulgare*). Smaller wild flowers can be grown in the shorter grass that forms the lawn, such as daisies, speedwell and dandelions. If you want a wild garden, you can forget about the rules and regulations involving weed control in lawns – the aim is to encourage them instead, although you will not have a pristine greensward to look out on.

Another advantage of a wildflower meadow as opposed to a neat lawn is that wild flowers tend to do better on poor soil, so you can dispense with otherwise necessary programmes of lawn feeding. If your soil is naturally rich, then mow your patch of grass, but remove the clippings to gradually impoverish the soil, which will allow

you to grow plants such as ox-eye daisies, knapweeds, columbines, mulleins and clover more easily. Wildflowers in meadow grass will attract bees and butterflies to your garden. Wild marjoram and thistle provide food in late summer, and clover is a great source of pollen for bees.

FLOWERS FOR A
WILD MEADOW

Achillea millefolium (yarrow)
Bellis perennis (field daisy)
Cardamine pratensis (cuckoo
  flower)
Centaurea cyanus (cornflower)
C. scabiosa (knapweed)
Cirsium aucule (dwarf thistle)
Genista tinctoria (Dyer's
  greenwood)
Knautia arvensis (scabious)
Leucanthemum vulgare (ox-eye
  daisy)
Papaver rhoeas (poppy)
Sanguisorba officinalis (salad
  burnet)
Primula veris (cowslip)
Ranunculus acris (buttercup)
Tanecetum parthenium (feverfew)
Taraxacum officinale (dandelion)
Veronica chamaedrys (Speedwell)

◁ This little wild corner has a number of naturally seeding plants, including foxgloves, primroses and scabious, among cottage garden favourites, such as pansies and phlox. An advantage of any wild flower garden is that it takes relatively little maintenance – a great bonus for busy city dwellers.

◁ This silver and white themed sunny patio has a handsome *Agave americana* in a stone urn as its focal point, surrounded by petunias, alyssum and valerian (*Centranthus ruber*), all plants that relish the sun. Variegated foliage plays a part in the silver theme, and helps to extend the season of interest.

PLANTS FOR BEES AND BUTTERFLIES

Achillea millefolium (yarrow)
Aster novae-angliae (Michaelmas daisy)
Buddleja davidii (butterfly bush)
Cardamine pratensis (cuckoo flower, lady's smock)
Centaurea cyanus (bluebottle, cornflower)
Digitalis purpurea (foxglove)
Dipsacus fultonum (teasel)
Epilobium angustifolium (rosebay willow herb)
Lavandula angustifolia (lavender)
Rudbeckia fulgida (black–eyed Susan)
Salvia officinalis (sage)
Solidago canadensis (goldenrod)
Symphytum officinale (comfrey)

Attracting wildlife

If you are going to include a pond in your garden, remember to make one side of it gently sloping so that wildlife, both birds and squirrels, can use it to drink from. You can use the spoil from a pond to make a small bank, which will provide good shelter for a variety of wildlife if you plant it with ground cover. (If you don't have a pond, supply a few shallow dishes of water as a drinking and washing place for birds.)

▷ This attractive informal garden is loosely planted with roses and groundcover, surrounding the small lawn. Informal planting schemes, such as this, take very little maintenance, although the grass will need cutting at fairly regular intervals. Paving or gravel, instead of a lawn, would reduce the work to a minimum.

WILD GRASS MIXTURES

Agrostis tenuis
Alopecurus pratensis
Anthoxanthum odoratum
Briza media (common quaking grass)
Cynosurus cristatus
Festuca rubra communta
F. r. rubra
Hordeum secalinum
Poa pratensis
Trisetum flavescens

The food that birds, bees and butterflies need can be divided into those that produce nectar and those that provide berries. Of the nectar-producing flowers, among the best to grow are clovers (*Trifolium*), thymes (*Thymus*), heathers (*Erica*), mulleins (*Verbascum*) and yarrow (*Achillea*). Rowan, hawthorn and holly trees are among the best berrying trees, and the following shrubs and trees also provide a positive feast of berries and seeds: cherry trees, honeysuckles, viburnum, privet (*Ligustrum valubaris*), pyracantha and cotoneaster. Of perennials, you could grow white bryony, wild arums – which have very handsome foliage, forget me nots – for their seeds, thistles and teasels.

A small woodland garden, or at least the inclusion of a few trees, will help to attract birds to your garden. Good trees to include would be birches, wild cherry trees (*Prunus avium*), crab apples (*Malus pumila*), hawthorns (*Crataegus*), elders (*Sambucus nigra*) and hornbeam (*Carpinus betulus*). The latter also makes a good hedge or windbreak for nests and could be used to screen the wild part of the garden from the more manicured area around the house. Under the canopy of trees you can grow the usual woodland plants, such as periwinkle (*Vinca*), celandines (*Chelidonium*), dogstooth violet (*Erythronium dens-canis*), primroses and violets, as well as some small foliage plants, such as *Tellima grandiflora* and *Epimedium*.

Plants for scent

▽ Among the best scented plants are roses, here surrounding a small seating area. Scented climbing roses, mingled with honeysuckles, are ideal candidates for this kind of setting.

Without question, if there is one attribute that no garden should be without, it has to be scent. Although so subtle as to pass unremarked occasionally, scent adds a magic ingredient to any garden, and is particularly valuable in a city garden as an antidote to the less attractive smells of pollutants of one sort or another.

Many plants are scented, and their fragrance is by no means restricted to the flowers. In some plants the leaves are deliciously scented or aromatic – sage (*Salvia*), thyme (*Thymus*) and mint (*Mentha*) among them. Herbs are among the best plants for scent and if you have a sunny corner of the garden, it is well worth growing a small selection (see pages 103-5 for suggestions as to the best culinary herbs). They are not only useful, but highly decorative too – good all-purpose plants for the small garden.

Roses and other scented climbers

If you ask anyone to name any scented plants that they can think of, roses are going to come high on the list. Indeed, there are so many different forms of scented rose, all exquisite, that it is hard to know which to choose. It helps, therefore, to have some idea of the different kinds of rose. Entire books have been written on rose classification,

◁ Wisteria does need a firm hand to keep it under control and to encourage flowering. The aim is to train the stems horizontally and reduce the flowering spurs to two or three buds. This is best done in two hits: once in late summer and again in mid-winter.

SCENTED SHRUBS AND CLIMBERS

Brugmansia (syn *Datura*)
   (summer)
Buddleja (summer)
Chimonanthus praecox (winter)
Daphne bholua, D. odora (winter)
Elaeagnus pungens (autumn)
Hamamelis mollis (winter)
Jasminum officinale (summer)
Lavandula (summer)
Santolina (scented foliage)
Salvia (scented foliage)
Magnolia grandiflora (summer)
Myrtus communis (summer)
Philadelphus 'Beauclerk' (late
   spring)
Rosa (summer)
Sarcococca (winter)
Syringa (late spring)
Viburnum x *bodnantense* 'Dawn'
   (winter)

but for the average novice gardener, it is sufficient to group them into climbers, bush roses and little patio roses, and to say that there are old roses, which have been grown for centuries, and more modern versions (of which the patio rose is one). The aim of modern breeding has been to get the best of all possible worlds – great scent, good looks, good habits – but despite all the efforts, some of the very old roses are still hard to beat. Everyone has particular favourites, but in a small garden you cannot go too far wrong if you concentrate on climbing roses, as they will give you the maximum amount of flower power and take up the minimum amount of space – at a premium anyway in the city garden.

There are many different types of climber, including huge rambling roses, such as 'Rambling Rector', 'Kiftsgate' and 'Bobbie James', which will happily scale any tree or building, reaching up to about 10m (30ft) or more. There are also more ladylike climbers, which will adorn the front or back of your house. Do be aware, however, that roses need plenty of sunshine, and they also like deep clay soil with plenty of good organic matter added to it. Among the most popular climbers for walls are 'New Dawn' – a relatively new delicate pale pink rose, and 'Marigold' – a loose-petalled semi-double very pretty yellow rose – both of which are well scented. The white, pink-tinged 'Madame Alfred Carrière', with double flowers that are also richly fragrant, is also a good bet. In addition to the roses with scented flowers, there is also the incense rose, *Rosa primula*, which has wonderfully aromatic leaves.

There are many other good scented climbing plants, not least among them the honeysuckles (although beware – not all species and varieties are scented). *Lonicera fragrantissima* is partially evergreen and has richly fragrant creamy white flowers in winter and early spring. *L. periclymenum* 'Serotina' is deciduous but is also highly scented. Jasmine has a very powerful scent; the white-flowered *Jasminum officinale*, in particular, can literally fill the garden with scent.

▽ Some magnolias are exquisitely perfumed as well as eye-catching, at a time of year when scent in the garden is in short supply. There is a wide range, of which the smaller forms, like *M. stellata* and *M. soulangeana,* are excellent for city gardens.

Scented shrubs and trees

It can be a great delight to have a winter-scented shrub in the garden. *Chimonanthus praecox*, or wintersweet as it is commonly known, has spicy scented flowers in pale yellow that appear on the bare branches in winter. *Hamamelis mollis*, the Chinese witchhazel, also has sweetly scented little yellow flowers on bare branches. *H. m.* 'Pallida' has dense clusters of paler yellow flowers flushed with red. Other good shrubs for winter scent are the pretty pinkish mauve flowered daphnes, such as *Daphne bholua*, and Christmas box (*Sarcococca*), with its small shiny green leaves and little white highly scented flowers.

Other good scented shrubs, for other seasons of the year, are mock orange blossom (*Philaldelphus*), which has clouds of highly fragrant white flowers; lilac (with white or mauve flowers, which are wonderful for cutting for the house); and the scented flowers of some of the viburnums, such as *Viburnum* x *burkwoodii.* As a star performer in a small space, grow the little magnolia, *M. stellata.* It has singularly beautiful starry white flowers in spring that are also highly fragrant. 'Royal Star' has bigger white flowers, and 'Rosea', pink flushed ones. If you have acid soil, you can grow some of the scented azaleas, among

◁ The heady scent of lilies, in particular that of Regale liles and these handsome pink striped Stargazer forms, as well as that of tobacco plants (*Nicotiana*) can be almost overpowering on a warm summer's evening.

SCENTED ANNUALS
PERENNIALS AND
BULBS

Convallaria majalis (spring)
Dianthus 'Mrs Sinkins' (summer)
Erysimum cheirii (spring)
Freesia (spring)
Hyacinthus (spring)
Iris unguicularis (autumn)
Lathyrus odoratus (summer)
Lilium 'Regale' (summer)
Malcolmia (summer)
Matthiola (summer)
Narcissus (spring)
Nicotiana (summer)
Pelargonium (some with scented
    leaves) (summer)
Primula (spring)
Thymus (scented leaves)

them the strongly fragrant *Rhododendron luteum*, which has rich yellow flowers in late spring and the added attraction of Autumn-tinted leaves as well.

For trees, some forms of ornamental cherry are scented, among them the Japanese cherry, *Prunus* 'Amanogawa', which is ideal for small gardens, and has semi-double scented pink flowers. The bird cherry, *P. padua*, has almond-scented white flowers in spring, as do *P.* 'Shirotae' and *P.* x *yedoensis*.

Other scented plants
There is also a wide range of scented perennials, bulbs and annuals to choose from. Among the most strongly scented are those in the carnation family, including pinks such as the old-fashioned 'Mrs Sinkins', stocks, (*Matthiola*), tobacco plants (*Nicotiana*) and bulbs, such as narcissus and freesias. No small garden should be without a short row of wallflowers, as there is nothing to beat their perfume on a sunny day in late spring. Sweet peas are also deliciously scented, and ideal for cutting for the house. Grow them up a wigwam to save space, or next to a fence. Lilies are among the strongest scented flowers, with a particularly rich, heady fragrance.

Edible plants

▽ Tomatoes are among the most satisfying edible plants to grow as they need relatively little space, but they must have a sunny corner and very generous supplies of water.

One of the greatest joys for any gardener is the thrill of picking home-grown produce, and nothing tastes more delicious than even the most gnarled carrot, if you have lovingly grown it from seed yourself! There is, of course, nothing to stop you from turning your whole small city plot into a kitchen garden, provided that it gets enough sun, and, if you want to grow vegetables, that you are prepared to put a lot of effort into ensuring that the soil is sufficiently rich in nutrients to support a good crop. Alternatively, you could grow just a small amount of produce in a corner of the garden of, if the fancy takes you, cottage style among the flowering plants.

Vegetables

The most important requirement for vegetables, apart from sunlight and water, is the soil that is rich in organic matter. One of the best ways of providing this is to make your own compost heap – an art in itself – from kitchen waste, plant clippings and so on (see page 112). Another point worth remembering if you are growing vegetables is that you need to rotate them according to type, ie root vegetables, brassicas and other crops, because if you grow the same crop in the same place year after year, diseases build up in the soil.

For a small garden, it is best to concentrate on plants that produce rewarding vegetables from a relatively small area of soil. Among the best are tomatoes, which can even be grown in special growing bags on a roof top or balcony; so too can lettuces and other small salad crops, such as radishes or spring onions. If you do not have much space, then look out for vegetables that offer particularly good flavour. Some of the more unusual tomatoes, or the little salad tomatoes, such as 'Gardener's Delight', are unfailingly good, taste

◁ Salad bowl lettuces, in red and green forms, can be used ornamentally as well as for their edible crop. They also make a pretty edging to a flower bed in summer. Curly parsley can also double as an attractive edging.

▽ This brightly coloured little herb garden has been formally designed, with lemon balm and calendula making the central feature, surrounded by marjoram and chives.

delicious, crop heavily and are easy to grow. Other good salad vegetables are beetroots, corn salad (also called lambs' lettuce), rocket (with a delicious spicy flavour), different kinds of lettuce – such as the Italian coloured curly lettuces like Lollo Rosso, and dwarf cos lettuces – Welsh onions and radishes.

You could grow any of the above in a neat square, with a brick surround, and perhaps even border the vegetable plot with a small brick path. If you wish, you could put a gooseberry bush, trained as standard, or a wigwam of runner beans, as a central point and make the beds as the four quarters of the square.

You can also plant globe artichokes (*Cynara scolymus*) in the back of a flower border – their silvery leaves and handsome purple-tinged heads (which you can eat) make a handsome statement of their own. The variety 'Gros Vert de Lyon' is a good eating form. Courgettes can be grown up a fence or trellis if you wish, but they need a rich soil and plenty of sunshine, as well as regular watering.

Culinary herbs

Whether or not you want to grow salad vegetables, it is well worth your while cultivating a few culinary herbs. Even if all the space you possess is a window sill in front of the kitchen window, you can manage to raise a few herbs, provided it gets some sun. Herbs are relatively easy to grow, and demand very little attention. Apart from in containers, the best position for them is by the kitchen door in a narrow border. Two or three of each kind will probably be more than enough for your needs. The following are among the best types to grow for culinary purposes:

▽ A narrow section of the garden has been devoted to an attractively organized vegetable and herb garden, with soldierly rows of parsley and spring onions, backed by beans and artichokes.

Basil There are two different kinds: bush basil and sweet basil. Sow seed out of doors after the last frosts.

Coriander Best grown in a border in drills about 30cm (12in) apart from seed sown in April, but the seed can be slow to germinate. You can use both the leaves of the plant, and the seeds, which will be ready in August.

Dill This is pretty enough to be grown in the flower border. The seed should be sown in April in drills about 30cm (12in) apart and the plants thinned out to a distance of about 23cm (9in). You can use both leaves and seeds.

Garlic If you enjoy garlic, it is not difficut to grow. Plant the cloves in autumn in a sheltered spot, at twice their own depth. They will be ready when the leaves start to fade. Store the bulbs hanging in bunches in dry conditions.

Marjoram There are several forms and it is most easily grown from rooted shoots from an existing plant. It is best to harvest the leaves before the plant flowers in July.

Mint This can be grown easily from root cuttings. Mint prefers richer soil to most herbs, and will also grow better in partial shade. It is inclined to spread, so either plant in containers or insert slates around the mint bed to prevent the roots running.

◁ Containers can provide a home for herbs, which are decorative as well as useful, as these terracotta pots of chives and purple-leaved sage (*Salvia purpurascens* 'Atropurpurea') demonstrate.

▽ Walls and fences can be used as a support for fruit, such as the cultivated blackberry ('Loch Ness') here, or cordons of fruit, such as apples and pears. Remember that the latter will need careful pruning if they are to bear good crops of fruit.

Parsley You can grow parsley from seed, twice a year in spring and late summer, but it is notoriously slow to germinate. It makes a pretty edging to a border and can also be used in containers as an edging plant (it looks good planted with blue pansies). It does best in light sandy soil. You can overwinter parsley in a cold frame to ensure you have some all year round.

Rosemary This is a pretty shrub, with bright blue flowers and small spiky aromatic leaves. It grows best in light soil in full sun. It grows easily and well from cuttings.

Sage There are many forms, some of which are simply flowering perennials, but the sage used for culinary purposes is *Salvia officinalis*. A deep purple form of this, 'Purpurascens', is particularly attractive. Grow it from cuttings in a sunny spot in light soil. You can harvest it for drying in mid-summer, but even if you don't, prune it back in late summer to prevent the bush becoming straggly.

Thyme This little bushy perennial comes in many forms, some of which are more pungently scented than others. They like a light, limy soil and are best grown from cuttings. Harvest the leaves for drying from early to late summer.

Fruit

There is plenty of room, even in quite a small garden, for some of the modern varieties of fruit, such as the cordon-trained apples or one of the family trees, with several delicious varieties grafted onto one tree. Peaches and nectarines can be grown in fan formation on a sunny wall, raspberry and blackberry bushes can be grown against a fence, and gooseberries trained as standards to add ornament to the vegetable plot.

Currant bushes are very prolific, and even just a couple will yield enough to make generous quantities of jam, for example. A fig tree, with it beautiful glossy grey-green hand-shaped leaves, can be grown in a large tub to make a handsome ornamental tree, which may just reward you with edible fruit if the climate is warm enough. Last, but by no means least, are grapes, which are well worth growing in any city garden. Provided you have a sunny aspect to the garden, a vine will reward you with beautiful foliage for a large part of the year, and the bonus of grapes (edible or for wine) in the autumn of most years.

CARING FOR YOUR GARDEN

IN ADDITION TO PLANNING, constructing and planting your garden, you need to know how to keep it looking good, so that you can enjoy it all year round. Not only do you need to choose appropriate plants and know how to maintain them in a healthy state – feeding, watering and pruning them as and when required – you also need to be able to increase your stocks of plants inexpensively by sowing seed or taking cuttings, for example. This chapter shows how, with the helpful addition of step-by-step illustrations. Although small city gardens require relatively low levels of maintenance, you will need to pay particular attention to feeding and watering, since plants in containers dry out very quickly and also have no natural replenishment of nutrients apart from what you, the gardener, supply.

◁ Build staging against the walls of a small garden to increase the planting space, and to give you a place to propogate your own plants.

▷ Every inch of space has been used in this garden, along with a range of containers, to get the greatest value from the garden. Herbs, perennials and annuals create a wonderful cottage-garden display.

Remodelling your garden

▽ Creating a small patio area for eating out can transform the way you use your garden. It is important to ensure that the area is surrounded by attractive planting that screens the area from prevailing winds.

If you have an existing city garden, you will need to decide what features are worth keeping and how you might adapt it to suit your needs better than it does already.

The problems faced by most city gardeners are inappropriate planting, inconveniently situated or overgrown trees and shrubs, and inadequate or unattractive surfacing. If you have an unlimited budget, it is feasible to solve all these problems at a stroke by hiring a garden designer, and getting him or her to deal with these problems on your behalf. Solutions will be dictated in part by the site and its limitations, in part by your taste and your own limitations of budget, and to a lesser extent by the designer's particular likes and dislikes.

The first question you have to ask yourself is what do you like about the existing garden, if anything? If there is a particularly attractive shrub or tree, or a good-looking patio, for example, then include these features in any proposals you make to alter the garden. A garden that is designed from scratch takes quite a while before it looks attractive in its own right, and a couple of well-grown shrubs or trees will help give it a more mature look much more quickly.

Aim for quality rather than quantity, and opt for a couple of major, interesting shrubs or trees rather than a

barrowload of unidentifiable bits and pieces from the garden centre. If you want flower colour, then fill up any unplanted spaces with some handsome annuals – tobacco plants (*Nicotiana*), for example, are ideal for this purpose. Cosmos, the big pink daisy-like perennial, will also grow from seed and is a good space filler while you wait for

shrubs to fill out and occupy their allotted space.

Make sure your planting spaces are generous enough and position plants at properly spaced intervals, having previously dug generous planting holes for them, and given them a good dose of fertilizer or bonemeal. Your garden, however well designed, will be

▷ A good basic core design is needed around which the planting can gradually take place. A good variety of plant types – shrubs, perennials and bulbs – will help to give depth and form to the garden.

ultimately only as good as the plants, and if you do not pay proper attention to their growing conditions – feeding, watering and light requirements – you will not be rewarded with a lush and handsome garden.

Most gardening books will tell you to draw up scale plans on paper before you plant, and you will certainly need to

draw up some kind of plan if you are ordering hard surfacing, as you need to estimate the cost and the quantity of material before you make the final decision. As far as the planting goes, in a small garden where most of it is likely to be visible from one standpoint, this is not strictly necessary, unless you plan to create quite complex borders. Most city

gardens, however, lack the space to imitate Jekyllesque flower borders, and you are unlikely to want to grow plants several rows deep, as in a traditional flower border. Background shrubs with a few smaller perennials in front, and perhaps a few bulbs for spring and autumn colour mixed in with them, are likely to be a more appropriate choice.

Buying & choosing plants

If you are planning a new garden, you will have to buy in stocks of plants, either by mail order or from your local garden centre or nursery. If you are not very experienced, the latter is the best solution as you can see precisely what you are getting and, if the nursery is a good one, there will be someone on hand to give you helpful advice. Do not be afraid to ask whatever questions you feel are necessary. Plant labels should give you basic information on size, flowering times and soil conditions, but you may well have other questions to raise – on pruning, perhaps, in the case of shrubs, or planting depths for bulbs, or whether particular plants will cope with the degree of shade or dryness, or whatever, in your garden.

When picking a plant from a nursery or garden centre, look for one with a good branch formation, unmarked fresh-looking leaves and no unusual blotches, holes or unnatural yellowing. Turn the pot upside down to check that the roots are not growing right through the base – a sign that the plant needs potting on. Do not be tempted by the plants currently in flower. Take a good look around, and check that the plant has several attributes, since with only a small space at your disposal, you want the maximum value for your outlay.

△ Mahonias, seen here in full flower, are among the top ten plants for the city garden. Evergreen, easy to grow, shade tolerant and with many forms with scented winter flowers, it is hard to beat.

Establishing soil type

It is important to establish the quality and type of the soil in your garden early on, as some plants can be notoriously fussy. Much as you may like camellias or azaleas, for example, you must have fairly acid soil for them, and you can find this out quite quickly and easily by

PLANNING THE PLANTING

• Make sure you have some evergreen shrubs or trees to provide a winter framework.
• Use climbers and wall shrubs to make the most of the vertical space.
• Buy generous size, handsome terracotta pots, rather than cheap plastic ones. Even unplanted, they look good.
• Make sure the plants you buy are appropriate for the situation.
• Group plants in three, five or seven of one kind to make a bold display. Do not dot individual small plants around.

doing a pH test on the soil. If you find that the soil is too acid or too alkaline, you can alter the pH by adding lime if it is acid or by adding peat if it is alkaline, but in general, particularly if you are fairly busy, you would be better advised to grow plants that like the conditions you have. In practice, most soil comes into the middle range in which most plants will do fairly well.

If the soil is very damp or very dry (the latter is more likely in the sheltered, shady environment of city gardens),

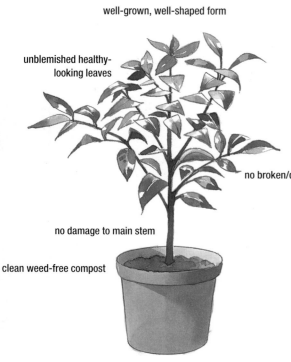

well-grown, well-shaped form

unblemished healthy-looking leaves

no broken/damaged branches

no damage to main stem

clean weed-free compost

no roots emerging from pot

▷ Another top rated plant for the city garden, *Fatsia japonica*, has many virtues. It grows fairly large, so reserve it for a corner of the garden – it will tolerate shade – to fill a blank space.

◁ Check that any plant you buy is growing strongly, that the shoots are healthy and unbroken, the leaves sound and unblemished, the compost weedfree and not sour-looking, and the plant, if it is a shrub, well formed.

then again there will be a limited range of plants that do well in it. You can examine the soil yourself by squeezing a good ball of it in your palm. If it is dry, gritty and the grains are well separated, you have a fairly sandy, naturally free-draining and therefore fairly dry soil. If they stick together in a lumpy mass, your soil has a hefty amount of clay in it, which means that it will not drain freely, becoming waterlogged in wet weather but drying out too quickly .

Whichever soil type you have, it will almost certainly be greatly improved by the addition of lots of organic material in the form of compost or of fertilizer. Clay soil will benefit from the addition of grit, to make it more porous, improving the oxygen content of the soil, which is important to plant health. Plant roots, surprisingly, require oxygen and will die off if they do not have an adequate supply. If you leave a plant too long in the pot in which you bought it, the roots will knit together into a ball and the plant will effectively die from suffocation. (The first signs will be that leaves wilt and yellow.)

From early spring onwards, the plants in your garden should start into healthy new growth. If this is not happening, then you have either planted them where they do not like the soil or situation, or they have an adequate supply of food or light. Aim to make sure that you give plants a good start. They need to be well looked after when young in order to form a healthy structure for later growth.

Planting, feeding & watering

It is important to make sure that you give your plants a good start when you plant them. They need, first and foremost, the right kind of soil and appropriate light conditions. There is no point in trying to get a heather or a rhododendron, for example, to grow in alkaline soil – they need the fairly acid conditions of their native habitats (see Buying and choosing plants).

Planting

Almost any plant will suffer shock as a result of being moved. It will recover more quickly and therefore grow better if the shock is minimized and the conditions are optimum. Be careful not to damage the fine feeder roots of the plants in the planting process; once the plant is in position these roots should be able to spread out and become operational, so make sure that you don't cram them into a planting hole that is too small, and that the surrounding soil is not too hard. Fork the area over, dig out a planting hole that is large enough for the roots to spread and grow into, firm the plant in well and water thoroughly. Thoroughly is the key word, since even apparently copious amounts of water only penetrate about an inch below the soil surface (as you will quickly discover if you insert a stick into the

soil in a container you have just watered).

Plants of any description do not like their roots moved, so if you are planting trees, make sure you stake the stems so that the rootball does not rock about as the result of wind movement on the stem. If you have to move plants, do so in the dormant season – in other words in autumn or early spring – and make sure you water them thoroughly.

Pruning after moving will help the plant establish itself more quickly.

Planting in containers

Most city gardens will have a few containers, and it is important that you know how to plant them and when and how to repot the plants (see also page 117). Choose a container that is approximately 20 per cent bigger than the root ball of the plant that is going to

---

MAKING A COMPOST HEAP

Making compost is actually satisfying and ecologically very sound, and you can buy purpose-made compost bins these days, which can be hidden away behind a small shrub. You can shred all your kitchen waste, garden clippings and leaves and so forth, and although it will not answer all your nutrient needs for the soil, it will certainly help. Simply add some compost activator to the pile occasionally, and with luck, in a few months, you will have some good, friable, organic matter to return to the soil.

A homemade bin can be made easily from a few wooden supports, with chicken wire nailed around them, as shown.

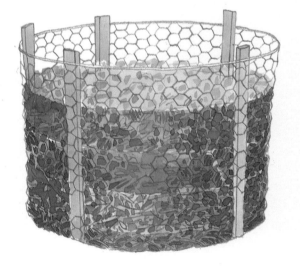

Planting a shrub

1 Dig over the ground to loosen the soil with a fork. Dig over a larger area than the planting hole so that the roots can penetrate the area easily.

2 If you are planting a container-grown plant, water it well before removing it from the pot. It will come out more easily.

3 Dig a large planting hole (at least twice the width of the rootball of the plant). Put in a little bonemeal or fertilizer to give the plant a good start.

4 Insert the plant in the planting hole, using a piece of wood if necessary to check that the plant is level with the surrounding soil surface.

5 Backfill the hole with soil, then tread around the plant carefully to firm it in, taking care not to damage the stem or roots.

6 Water thoroughly after planting and keep well watered until the plant is fully established.

be put into it. Too large a container will cause the plant to put on too much vegetation, and too small a container will cause the roots to wrap around the rootball, eventually choking the plant.

Any container should be clean before use, and should have a drainage hole, or holes, at the bottom. This is essential, as if water cannot drain away, it will stagnate, and the plant will rot in waterlogged conditions. To improve drainage and to prevent the compost blocking the drainage holes, cover the base of the pot with large pebbles or bits of broken clay pot. Then insert the compost until the depth of the base of the root ball, insert the plant, fill up with compost and firm down, inserting more compost if necessary. The top of the compost should be about 2.5cm (1in) below the rim of the pot to allow for room to water.

Feeding plants

One thing that very few plants are happy with, apart from a few stalwarts like ivy, is a soil that is very poor in nutrients. In a small city garden, the normal nutrient balance is often lost, either through water running off and leaching them away, or through inadequate plant debris enriching the soil. This is the main reason why plants in containers need copious

Planting in a container

1 Insert a drainage layer of stones into a clean pot, then add enough compost so that the top of the rootball will rest just below the rim of the pot.

2 Remove the plant from its previous container and insert it into the new prepared container.

3 Fill the pot with compost until it reaches just about 2.5cm (1in) below the rim of the pot (to allow space for watering).

4 Firm the plant in well and water thoroughly.

▷ A good collector's plant, *Abutilon megapotamicum* is an ideal subject for containers. It blends here beautifully with the purplish leaves of the vine, *Vitis vinifera* behind. Remember that container plants need regular feeding and watering.

artificial feeding, as you have to play the part that nature normally provides.

Generous quantities of fertilizer, spread over the garden in autumn, will help; make sure, if you have containers, that you do this on a regular basis throughout the growing season. Liquid fertilizers are the easiest to use for containers. Some plants require more than others; for example, if you want to grow edible plants such as tomatoes on a patio, they will need copious feeding and watering to produce a reasonable crop. (Tomatoes also need plenty of sunlight, so make sure you pick a suitably sunny spot.) Some of the Mediterranean plants that do well on poor sandy soil will do well with very little in the way of nutrients in the soil – pelargoniums, for example, will thrive on very little, and can become overly leafy if given too much fertilizer.

There are entire books devoted to the composition of fertilizers and certainly some plants will benefit from fertilizers with a particular balance of the ingredients that go into most multi-purpose fertilizers. As a general rule, be aware that potash is used for the formation of flowers and nitrogen for lush leaf growth, but in most cases you will do well enough with any proprietary fertilizer.

Plant tidying

If you have a small garden, it is very important that the plants look good at all times, as attention is focused on them so much more closely. You do need, therefore, to keep them in the best possible condition, firstly by offering them the right growing conditions and, secondly, by keeping them in good order.

Pruning and deadheading

Plants that climb and scramble will, in many cases, need to be tied to supports and pruned relatively regularly. Pruning some shrubs can be a fairly complex process if you are doing it in order to ensure the largest possible crop of flowers. However, if your main aim is simply to keep the plant healthy, in good condition, and within proper growing limits, then you can, in all cases, prune the plant directly after flowering. Remove about one third of the plant's growth, leaving a couple of outward-pointing buds from which the new shoots will grow. It is important that these buds are outward facing, otherwise the new growth will cross into the centre of the plant, eventually making an impenetrable thicket. (If you want to grow soft fruit in your garden with the aim of getting it to crop reasonably well for you, then this method is too simplistic.)

Basic pruning

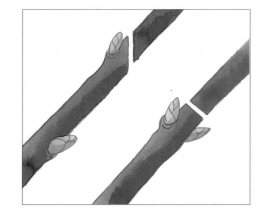

△ Prune shrubs where buds grow alternately with a diagonal cut just below the outward facing bud. Shrubs where the buds grow in pairs should be pruned straight acrsoss, just above a pair of buds.

Deadheading is important in order to keep the garden looking good, and to increase the crops of flowers. This seems like a chore, but it pays dividends because it encourages the secondary buds to develop and a whole new display of flowers, thus prolonging the flowering season, or in some cases, encouraging a second, later, display. Getting the most out of not a lot is the secret to successful city gardening, so it is worth arming yourself with a pair of sharp secateurs and snippng off any dead flowers neatly just below the base. This is particularly valuable with very floriferous plants, such as roses, unless

△ It is important when pruning to persuade the plant to grow outwards rather than in on itself. When pruning a shrub, make the pruning cut just above an outward-facing bud.

of course you want the value of the hips later in the year, in which case you can forego deadheading.

Although many gardening books will exhort you to cut all perennials down in the autumn, this is not really necessary. Although it was the rule of the day in big perennial borders, in city gardens it is nice to look at the display of seedheads in autumn, especially when they catch the frost, and does not do any real harm to the plant.

It will, however, pay to remove dead leaves in autumn. If you have the space, you can bag them up in black bin liners, puncture the bag with a few fork holes, and then allow the leaves to rot down over the winter before digging them back into the soil next spring. Or skip the lot and buy in commercial fertilizer, which is, at least, sterile.

Maintaining plants in containers
Plants in containers will need repotting every year or two, depending on their rate of growth. Examine the base of the pot periodically, and if the roots are beginning to grow through, then pot on into a pot about 20 per cent larger than the rootball.

If you have a plant that has become pot bound (that is, with the roots wound round the rootball), you may have to break the pot to remove it. If you do not pot it on into a bigger pot, it will slowly die, so it must be attended to. Remove the plant and then snip the roots back, freeing them as you do so, so that the roots are able to move outwards. Then pot into a suitably sized pot in the normal way.

If a plant is outgrowing its pot, and you do not wish it to grow any larger, restrict its growth by trimming back the roots by about one third of their length. You should also trim down the stems of the plant by about one third at the same time, and then repot into the original pot, from which the old compost has been removed and new compost added.

Repotting a container-grown plant

1 Check the base of the pot periodically to see if roots are beginning to emerge. Container plants will also need new compost every couple of years, even if slow growing.

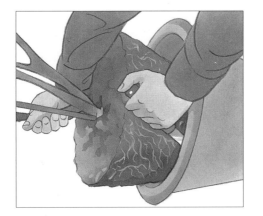

2 Remove the plant carefully from its pot. If necessary, you can use a knife to help ease it out, but be careful not to damage the roots in the process.

3 Gently tease out any wrapped around roots. If you want to stop a plant growing too big for its existing pot, trim the roots by up to one third.

4 Prune the plant if needed, and repot (see page 114) in a larger pot. The new pot should be approximately 5cm (2in) wider in diameter than the previous one.

Caring for plants in winter

It is often possible, in the microclimate of a city, to grow plants that would not normally survive in your particular climate. The proximity of buildings, the density of population and the amount of heat generated in a city often allow you to grow sub-tropical plants in a temperate climate – with some degree of caution.

Plants originating from hotter parts of the globe are, by and large, more exotic and more colourful than the native plants to cooler climates, and as container plants, they make wonderful additions to a city garden or balcony. Among those that you might consider are *Clivia miniata*, with its glossy green paddle-shaped leaves and scarlet flowers; the Abyssinian banana plant (*Ensete ventricosum*), with even bigger, similarly shaped leaves; the New Zealand tree fern (*Dicksonia antarctica*); and the trumpet vine (*Bignonia*), with its orange or scarlet clusters of flowers.

If you decide to risk growing these more exotic plants, you will need to take special precautions in cold spells in winter. One solution is to the wrap the plants in bubble plastic during particularly cold weather. If you cannot wrap the whole plant, then at least wrap the base of the container to keep the roots warm, as it is damage to the roots that will usually eventually kill a plant.

If you have the room, you may decide to move plants indoors in really frosty weather, but this can be a backbreaking task if the pots are large and heavy. Remember that a fully watered pot weighs at least twice as much as a dry one, so, if possible, let the pot dry out to some degree before trying to move it.

In the winter remove the remains of any annuals that have died, and recycle containers by removing and throwing away the compost, taking out the crocks and washing the container and the crocks before storing them for reuse. It is important to clean containers thoroughly before reusing them, as they can harbour diseases which may destroy new plants.

MOVING CONTAINERS

There are a few relatively simple methods for moving plants (which are also useful if you just want to reposition them in a sunnier or more prominent position, for example). One is to rock the pot onto the end of a heavy sack, and then to pull the sack along with someone helping you by holding the container. Another is to use a few metal rods and a couple of planks. Place the planks at right angles to four metal rods, lined up with about 7.5-10cm (3-4in between them and then, with two more planks providing a ramp, move the pot onto the plank platform. Then roll it along, moving the rods from front to back to provide a continuous rolling platform.

◁ *Clivia miniata* is an exotic plant that can actually survive in reasonably mild climates if its pot (or roots) are wrapped in winter with insulating material – bubble plastic is ideal. It has the bonus of beautfiul foliage, in a deep rich green, and clusters of striking crimson flowers.

wooden supports or windowboxes given a coat of wood preservative.

Maintaining Pools

Remove fallen leaves from a pool in autumn, or cover the pool with netting to prevent leaves getting into the water. (This is particularly important if you have fish, as decaying leaves will create toxic gases in the water.) As the leaves of aquatic plants end their life, break them off and remove them. Periodically reduce any oxygenating plants that are growing too vigorously.

It is essential that fish do not become trapped under ice, so if you live in a temperate climate, you may need to think about installing an electrical pond heater during cold winter months.

Cleaning a pool is best done during early summer. If you have fish, remove them, with some of the water, to a bucket or other container. Scoop out any plants and divide them if necessary. Empty the pool, then scrub the pool sides, and refill, with clean water. Fish need to be acclimatized gradually, so leave the bucket standing in the pool for a few hours before releasing the fish into the clean water.

Water pumps and fountains will need to be serviced regularly if they are not to become clogged, and the filter will need to be kept clean and free of debris.

Winter is a good time to carry out any basic maintenance on the patio. Pick a pleasant day, when it is not too cold, and give all the furniture and the patio surface a good clean. A wire brush and algaecide (or even household detergent) will remove any lichen deposits on wooden furniture and decking. If you have a vacuum cleaner that will cope with wet and dry, you can also give a patio or balcony a good clean through to remove the build up of grime that is inevitable in most cities. Painted furniture can be repainted and any

Increasing the stock

If you have any space at all to plant, you are probably keen to fill it with plants, and it can be expensive to do so if you buy it all in from the garden centre, so it is helpful to know how to increase the plants you already have.

There are three principal methods: using the seed of the plant, using the stems and leaves, and using the roots or bulbs. Plants are very accommodating and some will allow you to use more than one method to get them to create offspring.

In general, annuals and some perennials are sown from seed; perennials can also be increased, in many cases, by dividing their roots, if they have a clump-forming habit; and shrubs are normally increased from cuttings taken from the tips of stems. Some plants reproduce themselves with consummate ease, while others take a great deal more nurturing to do so.

It is useful to know which ones are particularly easy, as you can save yourself a lot of time and heartache by concentrating your energies on those that reward you easily and prolifically. With pelargoniums, all you have to do is remove a small tip of the stem with a few leaves and a shard of the actual stem from one of the sideshoots, make a hole with a dibber in a small pot of compost,

Taking softwood cuttings

1 Fill a suitable sized container almost to the brim with compost, and make small holes to receive the cuttings around the rim of the pot.

and insert the removed shoot, keeping it well watered. If you take half a dozen of these, you will be rewarded in a relatively short space of time (a maximum of six weeks) with half a dozen new pelargonium plants. Late summer is the best time to do this, but you will need the space to overwinter your new progeny.

Other plants that take easily from these kind of cuttings are box (*Buxus sempervirens*) and rosemary (*Rosmarinus officinalis*), both of which strike extremely easily from cuttings, without much help from the

2 Remove side shoots from the main stem of the parent plant using a sharp knife.

3 Insert cuttings in the pot and firm in well. Water well, add supporting stakes and place a clear polythene bag over them to retain moisture.

Sowing seeds in trays

1 Fill a seedtray with proprietary seedling compost to within about 2cm (1in) of the brim.

2 Tamp the compost down with a flat board with a handle to create a firm surface.

3 Scatter the seed, or sow it in fine drills, according to type. A folded sheet of paper serves as a useful means of controlling the flow of seeds.

4 Cover the seeds with a sieved layer of compost (the thickness depends on the size of the seed – fine seed is barely covered, for example).

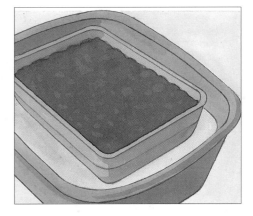

5 Stand the compost tray in a bowl of water so that it is watered from the bottom up, which will ensure it is moistened through all its layers.

6 Cover the tray with a sheet of glass, or clear plastic film, to preserve moisture. Compost should be moist, but not wet, until the seeds germinate.

◁ Tobacco plants (*Nicotiana*) make the ideal space filler in a small garden, growing rapidly and easily from seed each year. Not only do they look good, they have a wonderful scent, each evening.

five or six seed to a pot and will need a support to climb over), both of which give a good display in the garden or even in a large container.

Follow the manufacturer's instructions on the packet as to depth of sowing, but remember that the seeds must be watered lightly and regularly or they will not thrive. If you allow the seeds to become waterlogged, the seedlings may rot, and if they become too dry, they will simply wither and die. They will also need a good supply of even light; if they are on a window sill, turn them periodically so that they do not grow towards the light. Place a piece of glass or plastic wrap over the tray or pot to help conserve moisture and increase the warmth that most seeds need to germinate.

Once the seedlings are of a reasonable size (big enough to hold in your fingers), you can prick them out (transplant them) into a larger container or into their place in a bed or border.

Dividing plants

Clump-forming perennials, and most bulbous plants, can be increased by division, either of the roots, in the case of fibrous rooted perennials, or by pulling off new small bulblet from the main bulb, in the case of bulbs.

propagator. Osteospermums, the glistening white daisies, will also do well from cuttings, as will penstemons and hydrangeas.

Sowing seeds

You need only arm yourself with a few small pots and a couple of plastic trays with drainage holes in the bottom, and some seed and cuttings compost to try your hand at raising plants from seed. There are many annuals and some perennials that grow easily from seed. Among the most satisfying are tobacco plants (*Nicotiana*), and particularly the 2m (6ft) giant tobacco plant, *Nicotiana sylvestris*, and sweet peas (which are best planted in a fairly deep pot with

Division of roots is relatively easy; you simply have to take a look at the plant and see if it has more than one main growing stem coming from a basal clump. If it does, you can split the plant and replant both pieces (or more than two if the plant is large) to grow on into separate plants. Whether or not you want more plants, large clump-forming perennials will benefit from being divided every few years to give them a new lease of life.

Bulbs will usually produce offsets, and the time to take them off is normally in the autumn (for spring-flowering bulbs), when the new small bulbils will have formed. It will normally take more than one season for these to produce new flowering shoots.

It is important, for many bulbs, that you allow the dying leaves to stay on the plant after flowering, as these feed back into the plant to build up next year's stock of flowers, so do not be tempted to simply cut them off after flowering.

Tuberous plants, such as irises, can be propagated by cutting the tuber into smaller portions, provided each new portion has a growing point from which a new stem can emerge. Irises, unlike most plants, need very little soil covering the tubers, and should be planted only just below the level of the compost.

Dividing plants

1 Most plants are best divided in autumn. Trim away any dead or dying foliage with a pair of secateurs.

3 Either replant the clump, or divide again, into selected roots with growing points.

2 Using two forks back to back, divide the clump by pushing down and away on the forks. Smaller clumps can be divided with two hand forks.

4 Into prepared soil, plant the newly divided plant, firming it in well and watering it thoroughly.

Plant-shaping techniques

Plants that have been trained or trimmed into more architectural shapes can look very attractive, and make an excellent visual statement at the top of a flight of steps, on a porch or balcony, if positioned in pairs.

You can grow plants as standards – in other words remove the lower stems so that the plant bushes into a neat round at the top of a tall, bare stem – or clip or train the branches of evergreen shrubs into topiary shapes, such as cones, balls, squares, or whatever you prefer. You can buy frames for more elaborate shapes, but be warned that these require very well-grown plants, which must be kept in excellent condition.

There are a number of plants that adapt well to being grown as standards, among them the shiny leaved bay tree (*Laurus nobilis*) and myrtle (*Myrtus communis*) and flowering shrubs such as some roses, honeysuckles and fuchsias, which form a wonderful, flower-packed ball in summer. The method is the same for either.

Topiary shapes can be trimmed quite easily provided they are relatively simple. Grow the plant in a container (either from a cutting or seed) and when it has reached a reasonable size – say about 23cm (9in) above the soil and with a few stems – pinch the growing points out to encourage it to bush out.

Training a standard

1 Once the newly shooting plant has reached about 30cm (12in) in height, you can start to remove some of the lower side shoots. Tie the plant to a stake to support it.

2 Once the plant has reached the appropriate height, pinch out the bud from the leading shoot to stop all further additions to the height.

3 Pinch out some of the top shoots as they emerge to encourage further bushy secondary growth, so the top head of the plant bushes out.

4 The fully grown, trained standard. Foliage standards, clipped as topiary, will need a twice a year shearing. Dead head flowering standards as the flowers die back.

◁ A variegated ivy has been trained up a spiral frame in a container. Ivy is the poor man's topiary, quickly creating architectural shapes that it would take several years to produce with more classical topiary plants, such as box or yew.

The following season you can start to clip it into shape, by placing a simple wire frame (known as a batten) over the plant, and then trimming off the protruding leaves and stems. This should be done twice a year, in spring and in late summer. Feed and water the plant well in the growing season to encourage healthy leaves to form.

A simpler version can be made with ivy, grown over a frame. Simply grow a few ivy plants (it grows perfectly well from cuttings with a few roots attached to the stem) around the edge of a terracotta pot. Insert the frame over the pot, to fit inside the rim, and then train the trailing ivy stems over the frame. Once it has filled out you can start to trim the ivy to shape with secateurs until it completely fills the frame, making its own topiary shape.

Training an ivy pyramid

1 Find a suitable wire frame – pyramid, cone or ball – and a pot – ideally a good quality terracotta one – into which it fits comfortably .

2 Plant up the ivy – ideally two or three small plants around the perimeter of the pot – and place the frame over it.

3 As the shoots grow, tie them into the sides of the frame with plastic ties and encourage the leading stems to climb up the frame.

4 In a relatively short time, the ivy will cover the frame. Keep it clipped with garden shears a couple of times a year to preserve the shape.

Index

Picture Credits

All pictures in this book were supplied by **The Garden Picture Library**. Photographers and, where known, designers, are credited by page number and, where necesary, position on the page: (B) Bottom, (T) Top, (L) Left, (R) Right.